THE SOUL OF A SHOEMAKER

THE STORY OF FRANK KATANA'S DARING ESCAPE FROM COMMUNIST YUGOSLAVIA, HIS RISE TO FREEDOM, AND HIS JOURNEY TO SUCCESS

SUSAN CORK

The Soul of a Shoemaker © 2022 by Susan Cork.
All rights reserved.

Published by Author Academy Elite
PO Box 43, Powell, OH 43065
www.AuthorAcademyElite.com

All rights reserved. This book contains material protected under international and federal copyright laws and treaties. Any unauthorized reprint or use of this material is prohibited. No part of this book may be reproduced or transmitted in any form or by any means, electronic or mechanical, including photocopying, recording, or by any information storage and retrieval system, without express written permission from the author.

Library of Congress Control Number: 2022916940

Paperback: 979-8-88583-132-1
Hardback: 979-8-88583-133-8
Ebook: 979-8-88583-134-5

Available in hardback, paperback, e-book, and audiobook

Any Internet addresses (websites, blogs, etc.) and telephone numbers printed in this book are offered as a resource. They are not intended in any way to be or imply an endorsement by Author Academy Elite, nor does Author Academy Elite vouch for the content of these sites and numbers for the life of this book.

Some names and identifying details have been changed to protect the privacy of individuals.

Dedication

For my parents Frank and Ljubica

Preface

For many years I wanted to write my father's story. When an opportunity came to put his story on paper, I thought it may have been too late because of extraneous circumstances. However, this did not stop me from gathering all his stories from my mother, my brother, and various family members from Croatia to publish his story.

I had initially planned to write my father's memoir to share how he escaped communist Yugoslavia and his journey to Canada with my family and friends. Then I realized his story was more relevant today than at any other time in our history. We have been in this never-ending pandemic for years, and there seems to be no end to our country's mandates and government control over its citizens.

The current federal and provincial governments have imposed draconian restrictions on how we are to live and work in our beautiful country. My father left everything behind to escape from a brutal regime. He believed he would have a better life for himself and his family if he could have the opportunity to thrive in a free country. Many of the current measures taken by our governments resemble, in both form and function, the authoritarian policies that my father risked his life to escape from in Yugoslavia. Today, I see how vital it is to tell his story as our government continues to control our lives by enforcing many mandates, unlike before in our lifetime in Canada.

THE SOUL OF A SHOEMAKER

As my father grew up, he struggled to survive and worked hard in a country of oppressive restrictions under the guise of prosperity and equality for all comrades. He never gave up and took risks that could have put him in prison or had him executed because he wanted freedom. His journey to freedom, his sacrifices, and his love for family is the story I wanted to tell. His origin story is unlike any other I had ever heard of, and I felt it was important to share.

Prologue

Summer of 1956

Frank Katana could taste the blood from his split lip as he lay face down on the train compartment floor. Everyone around him shifted away in their seats to avoid drawing attention to themselves.

How many others on this train were attempting to flee Yugoslavia?

It was a dangerous gamble Frank had undertaken. Make it, and he'd have the innumerable choices that came with freedom. However, if he were caught, it meant a stint in one of Tito's infamous prisons.

Frank felt the officer's fingers tighten around his foot and kicked back hard to escape his clutches. It was no use. That burly man with a scar running down his left cheek had a death grip on his left shoe. Looking over his shoulder, he considered just losing the shoe, but he'd need it for what lay ahead. That is if he could get off this train before they arrived at the next station, where this brute could call for backup.

Frank kicked out again and again as the man pulled on his leg. Now the man had a vice grip on his calf, and his clawlike hand was attempting to climb further up his leg. Frank continued to kick, delivering blow after blow to the man's head and arm. He doubted his soft leather shoes were doing much damage. However, one of the blows struck the man squarely on the nose, and he yelped in pain and loosened his grip long enough for Frank to wriggle free.

He felt a momentary pang of guilt when he saw the torrent of blood pouring from the man's nostrils. Still, he had no time to ponder the damage. This was his one chance, and he needed to take it. Frank scrambled to his feet and ran for the connecting door. He opened it and stepped onto the platform between the cars. The train lurched and Frank grasped the handrail. He swiveled and hit the cold metal of the door, groaning. How close he'd come to being pitched into the night air.

However, the reality was that he'd have to jump. There was no way around it.

Frank tensed in fear at the prospect. He steadied himself and looked back through the door's window. The officer had made it to his feet. The man was clutching a rag against his nose, calling for backup on his radio.

How many other police officers were on the train? It was hard to tell. Frank knew there were more, but it was a long train with lots of compartments. He hoped it would take some time for the other officers to arrive. Frank felt the cool evening breeze hit his face. He was thankful the sun had set just moments ago. At least that was in his favor. He'd need the cover of darkness if he were going to be successful—if he were truly going to try to make it to the other side of the border.

Frank felt a sharp pang deep in his chest as he thought of his friends Luka and Petar. They'd planned to escape together, but neither friend had a convincing story to explain their presence on the train so close to the border. So the police had forced them off the train at the previous station. Maybe they'd just be sent home. That did happen on occasion. However, more likely, they would end up rotting in one of the many prisons set up for the traitors to Tito. Either way, they'd be roughed up.

PROLOGUE

Frank shook his head in an attempt to rid himself of the nightmarish thoughts. He didn't have time to mourn his friends' fate at this moment. No, he had to keep his eyes on his goal.

He had to get off this train.

The train banked hard and slowed with a high-pitched whine of the brakes. Frank clapped his hands over his ears and fell back against the door. He glanced back through the window and gasped as he saw the officer's hand on the door handle. The man's look of pure hatred made Frank flinch and take a step back. If caught, this man would surely see that Frank spent the rest of his days regretting his actions.

He had to do something.

Now.

The train continued to slow down as it navigated the large turn. The officer's hand reached out just as Frank leapt into the darkness. He heard the officer shout at the top of his lungs, "*Jebote!*"

Frank smiled as he flew through the air. He hit the ground and tucked and rolled to a stop. He allowed himself a moment to catch his breath, then heaved a sigh of relief. He'd made it off the train in one piece.

Now he just needed to find the border before the dozens of police officers and their snarling dogs found him.

Chapter One

Fall of 1940

Frank opened one eye and sighed. He wondered if it was time to get up. He tilted his head to the right and listened to his older brother Josip snoring away. He held his breath and waited a moment. Had it been his imagination, or had he heard the avian alarm clock cry out? He rolled over and closed his eyes again.

As if answering his question, the rooster crowed again, causing Josip to sit up and rub his eyes.

"Time to get up, lazy bones," his brother said with the cheerfulness of a natural-born farmer. "The chickens are waiting."

"Let them wait," Frank grumbled, but he got up. His morning chores wouldn't get done by themselves. A cool breeze kissed his ankles as he quickly donned his well-worn cotton pants and shirt.

He made a quick trip to the outhouse. Stepping inside, he groaned at the fat spiders who treated the room as their home. He shooed away two before he sat down and did his best not to imagine what lurked under the cracked wooden seat.

After washing his hands, he picked up the feed bucket and headed to the chicken coop. How he wished he had a little brother or sister to take over this task. He sighed as he opened the small door, ducked his head, and stepped inside.

"Ouch, ouch!" Frank cried as two chickens pecked at his ankles in anticipation of their breakfast. His thin shoes and socks offered little protection against their sharp beaks.

He poured the food into their feeder as quickly as possible, trying not to spill too much on the hay-strewn ground. He then collected the eggs. It was a good haul of ten, and *Majka* would be pleased.

Frank brought the eggs into the kitchen, put them on the table, and headed out to the barn. On the way he paused to enjoy the brilliant colors in the sky as the sun peeked over the horizon. Then he entered the barn to muck the stalls. His nose wrinkled at the smell of *sranje*.

Frank paused as a family of mice scurried over his feet. Where was that lazy cat? He'd gotten fat from over-feasting on the plethora of rodents that lived in the Katana home. At least the house had fewer furry visitors than the barn.

Finally done with his chores for the morning, he washed up in the basin by the front door. The pitcher was nearly empty, so he went to the well to fill it up for Josip, who would be coming in shortly.

"Come for breakfast," *Majka* called out.

He grinned at his mother's voice. "Yes, *Majka*," Frank said eagerly.

He sat down at the circular pine dining table next to his brother. *Majka* would sit between Frank and his father, Ivan, when she was done serving. Stjepan and Yoshka sat next to Ivan. His two uncles had come to live with them last year. Father needed help with the farm, and they needed a new place to live after a storm had plowed a tree through the roof of their home. Beside them sat Valentin, Frank's grandfather, and next came Josip.

As soon as Frank sat down, his mother put a plate of heaping scrambled eggs in front of him. Then she placed a small dish of homemade yogurt next to it.

CHAPTER ONE

Frank scooped a spoonful of *šipak* jam that *Majka* had just made into the creamy white yogurt and dug in.

Stjepan plucked a feather from Frank's back and handed it to him. "A gift from one of your friends," he said with a grin.

Frank let the feather fall to the floor. "Not exactly friends," he muttered.

"Farming isn't the life for you?" his uncle said with a twinkle in his eye.

Frank put his fork down and looked Stjepan in the eye. "No, not really. I've been thinking."

"About what?"

"I think I want to learn to be a cobbler."

"Ho, a cobbler?" his father said. "You're going to need a lot of training for that."

Frank sat up straight in his chair. "I know."

"Years," his father continued. "And there's no skilled shoemaker in Mali Bukovec. You'd have to go to Ludbreg. That's fifteen kilometers."

Frank nodded. "I can ride my bike."

"You've got to finish school first," *Majka* said.

"I know. I only have another four years. When I'm twelve, I can start."

They all fell silent for a moment. Frank continued to eat as he watched his mother move around in the kitchen. His eyes fell on his grandfather, who was studying him carefully.

"I think it's a good idea," his grandfather said quietly. "It's a good trade. Learn it well—it's a skill that will serve you well. You'll never go hungry."

Frank beamed. "That's what I thought."

* * *

Frank hefted his book bag over his left shoulder as he trudged along the dirt road to the small one-story school in the center of Mali Bukovec. It was a short walk, but the heavy load made him switch shoulders numerous times. It didn't help that the wild geese were constantly underfoot.

As Frank approached the front steps, he spotted his friend Jelik jogging up to meet him from the right. Frank stopped to wait for his friend so that they could enter the building together.

Jelik gave him an anxious look and ran a hand through his curly brown hair. "Are we late?" he whispered.

Frank shook his head. "I don't think so. I left at the same time I always do." He hoped he was right. You didn't want to be late for Miss Grzanic's class.

"Good," Jelik said, exhaling as if he'd been holding his breath. "Did you get the math done?"

"Yeah. It took me over an hour, but I did it."

"Me, too. I can't stand long division."

Frank and Jelik walked up the roughly hewn stone steps and into the cool interior of the old brick building. The dimly lit hallway was bustling with children ducking into the various classrooms.

As they walked into the second room on the right, Frank looked up at the large black and white clock on the wall. He grinned, relieved to confirm they still had seven minutes before class began. To say that Miss Grzanic didn't look kindly upon tardiness was an understatement. He'd only been late once, and he was determined not to repeat that error. He remembered the burn on his backside from the paddling he'd received, and his cheeks flushed from embarrassment.

Frank and Jelik slid into their small wooden desks that were side by side and waited. The room was only half filled with children, but over the next few minutes more filed in and took their seats. Only one chair remained empty.

Vinko's chair.

Frank stared at the clock. Two minutes to go.

CHAPTER ONE

Miss Grzanic walked in, and her blond hair was pulled back in a tight chignon. Her long angular face was accentuated by a pair of black eyeglasses. She frowned slightly as she looked out over the students. Frank could tell that she was counting the children. When her gaze fell on the empty seat, she grimaced and sat down.

One minute.

Jelik and Frank exchanged nervous glances. Neither liked Vinko, but they hated seeing any of their fellow students beaten. With every thwack of the paddle, Frank's backside hurt in sympathy.

The second hand seemed to race around the clock face too quickly. Just before it hit twelve, Frank turned to stare at the door. No Vinko. Maybe he was sick?

Miss Grzanic's eyes darted to the door before she called roll. Once done, she put the clipboard away and started the class off with geography. There was a hushed shuffling sound as each child brought out their notebook and began writing the capital city for each country listed on the front board.

Frank had practiced until bedtime and was confident he knew the capitals of all the countries in Europe.

Ten minutes later, the door squeaked open, and all the students turned to stare at a red-faced Vinko. He studied the floor as he shuffled to his seat, his bulky frame hunched as if he thought he could shrink and arrive unnoticed.

Frank glanced at the teacher. Miss Grzanic cleared her throat in a way that made Frank cringe. Everyone knew what that sound meant, including Vinko. He groaned, dropped his book bag by his desk, and went to the front of the classroom.

"I-I'm sorry I-I'm late, Miss Grzanic," he said, his voice low and trembling. "My chores went longer this morning. We had to pick the apples from our tree. It's market day. I ran all the way here."

"There's no reason you couldn't have arrived on time," she said with a slight shake of her head. "Vinko, you know what to do," she continued quietly. She then stood up from her desk and went to the hook by the side of the blackboard which held a thin, rectangular paddle. She gripped it with her right hand and turned to face Vinko, who hadn't moved.

She gestured to him to lean over her desk. His eyes darted around the room as if he might consider fleeing. He took two heavy steps and gripped the side of her desk, leaning in.

Miss Grzanic brought back the paddle.

Thwap!

Frank knew Vinko well enough to know that the last thing he wanted to do was cry out in pain, so when the high-pitched cry reverberated through the room, Frank recoiled.

Thwap, thwap!

Vinko slumped against the desk, moaning.

"You may go to your seat," Miss Grzanic said softly.

Miss Grzanic waited for Vinko to be seated. When he sat back down, he moaned softly. Frank winced, knowing the soreness the boy felt.

Slapping the paddle against her hand, the teacher took a deep breath. "Lateness cannot be tolerated. It is a sign of weakness. Be like our brave leader—loyal and honest citizens. Remember, you are all pioneering builders of the future. Work hard, love our homeland, and labor together in brotherhood and unity to spread these principles upon which this great country was built."

Frank suppressed the urge to roll his eyes as she continued to extol the leader's virtues. He knew she was talking about Josip Tito, who had recently assumed the presidency of the Communist Party of Yugoslavia. Lately, many people had been joining this movement in the hopes of bettering their lives. Frank had listened to lively discussions around the dinner

CHAPTER ONE

table as his family debated how the principles would affect their livelihood and lives.

Frank watched as the teacher smacked the paddle back in its spot on the wall. The children's eyes stayed riveted on the swaying slice of wood.

"So class, it's time to study hard." Miss Grzanic walked around the room and collected the homework. The children worked on their handwriting as they waited anxiously for their teacher to grade the pages. They knew poor grades also could be grounds for punishment. Frank had worked hard and hoped that Miss Grzanic at least appreciated the effort he'd put in.

While passing the assignments back, she paused at Frank's desk and smiled. "You did well, comrade. Again. Good job," she said before she continued onward.

As the teacher continued to pass homework out to students, Frank realized he was the only one to receive praise. The other kids received their work back in silence, some with a slight nod, while others were the recipient of a frown that made them tremble in their seats.

Frank's breath caught in his throat when Miss Grzanic practically threw Vinko's homework at him with a disapproving glare and a disgusted shake of her head. The pages were filled with red marks. Embarrassed, Vinko clutched the paper to his chest and looked around. Noticing Frank's eyes on him, Vinko glowered menacingly at him. Frank quickly looked away and shifted uncomfortably in his chair. He picked up his pencil and wrote a series of very shaky letters.

Chapter Two

It was just after two when the school bell rang. Frank eagerly grabbed his books and shoved them into his bag, then turned to Jelik, who'd done the same.

"Come on," Jelik said, jumping up and racing for the front door.

Although Frank knew his parents expected him home soon to do his afternoon chores, he wasn't eager to return to the farm. Whatever Jelik had in mind was probably more fun.

"I'm hungry," Frank said.

"Me, too. I have an idea!"

Frank followed Jelik as he raced out the school's front door. "Where are we going?"

"You'll see."

They ran past a gaggle of geese and, on the outskirts of town, Jelik took a rutted path along a corn field. After a few minutes, he stopped in front of a large apple tree.

Frank's mouth watered as he stared at the deep red apples hanging from the tree. "I don't know."

"No one will find out," Jelik said as he grabbed an apple and bit into it. His eyes closed in sublime pleasure. "It's so sweet."

"It's just I don't think Farmer Krajl will like it," Frank said.

"This is the Krajl farm?" Jelik said, pausing midbite. "I didn't know."

"Yeah," Frank said, pulling an apple from the tree. "But you're right. He won't find out."

CHAPTER TWO

They munched on the apples, and both picked another before they began walking back towards the village. In the distance, Frank saw the shape of three boys approaching. As they got closer, he recognized that one of the boys was Vinko.

"Where did you get that from?" Vinko bellowed, indicating the apple in Frank's hand.

Frank gulped. In his hands was the evidence of his theft from the boy's family farm. "I…uh…" His voice trailed off as he realized he had nothing to say.

"Oh, come on," Jelik said. "The tree was full of fruit. It won't miss a few."

"It might not. But I will," Vinko said, carefully putting his book bag to the side of the path. He rolled up his sleeves. "Your farm is on the other side of town. You came this way on purpose to steal those apples from me."

Frank felt the twinges of fear creep up his spine as he eyed the two other boys that had accompanied Vinko. They had placed their bags next to his and were obviously preparing for a fight.

"It's too bad about what the teacher did to you," Frank said quietly.

Vinko turned crimson and growled. Instantly Frank realized his mistake in bringing up the incident. Vinko lunged at Frank.

"You steal from me, I steal from you," he said as he knocked Frank to the ground. Since he weighed at least a stone more than Frank, Vinko had an easy time subduing him. For a third grader, the boy was large.

The other two pinned Jelik down and watched their leader.

Vinko pulled Frank's right shoe off and looked at the other two, who grabbed Jelik's left shoe. Once they had the prize, the two stood up, but not before punching Jelik in the stomach for good measure.

"Now we're even," Vinko said, standing up.

"How's that even?" Frank asked, panic rising in his throat. He couldn't lose his shoe, not with winter approaching. And he couldn't ask his parents for another pair. *Majka* had just bought these last month.

"You want it back?" Vinko said, standing up. He took Frank's shoe and twisted it back and forth until the heel came off. He threw the piece as far as he could, then tossed the shoe back to Frank. "There."

Vinko's friends did the same with Jelik's shoe. Frank could tell that Jelik was fighting back tears, but to his credit, his friend remained silent. The two watched the bullies walk away before either of them spoke.

"What am I going to do?" Jelik moaned. "My father will be so furious. There's no cobbler in Mali Bukovec. *Majka* will have to go all the way to Veliki Bukovec."

"I think that was the idea," Frank muttered. "Since it's two kilometers to get to the cobbler in Veliki Bukovec, it'll take days until we get our shoes back."

After retrieving the two heels, the boys hobbled back toward town, each deep in thought. About halfway there, Frank said, "Let me try to fix the shoes."

"You can do that?" Jelik asked, his eyes widening in wonder. "If you can repair my shoe, that would be fantastic."

Frank nodded. "I think I can."

"You're a life saver!" Jelik said.

* * *

Frank glanced at the house before he jogged over to the large barn. As he entered, he slowed and allowed his eyes to adjust to the darkness. He looked around his father's workbench until he found tiny nails and a small hammer. His heart raced as he looked over his shoulder. He didn't want to explain the incident to his parents and prayed no one would catch him

CHAPTER TWO

in the act of fixing his shoe. After all, *Majka* had told him on other occasions that stealing apples from another farm wasn't acceptable.

He was glad to have found the nails. There were a few dozen there. Frank figured that he could get away with six nails for each shoe. His father wouldn't miss them. And if needed, he could always add a few more later.

Frank pursed his lips as he tapped the little nails into the heel of his shoe and then into Jelik's.

He tested the shoes and was relieved when the heels stayed firmly in place. He grinned and put the tools back where he'd found them. No trace he'd ever been there.

When he walked through the front door, he smelled the delicious *knedle*. His stomach growled in anticipation of the flavor of the plum dumplings. No one made *knedle* like his mother.

"How was school today?" she asked.

"Good," he said with his mouth full. "I have some homework. After, can I visit Jelik?"

She shook her head. "Father needs your help with the sugar beets as soon as you're done with your work."

"Yes, *Majka*," he said. "It's just that I need to bring him something. It's important."

She turned from the stove and looked at Frank. "Did he forget his homework assignment again?"

Frank nodded at the white lie. "If I don't bring it to him, he'll be in trouble." Well, that part was true. Frank didn't even want to imagine his friend's punishment if Jelik's father learned that he'd lost his shoe.

"Well, you'd better go now," she said with a sigh. "Just come back as fast as you can. We don't want the sugar beets to rot."

"Yes, *Majka*," Frank said, shooting up out of his chair. "I'll run. I promise."

THE SOUL OF A SHOEMAKER

* * *

The large round pine table seemed so small as the Katana family crowded around for dinner. Frank watched as *Majka* ladled out the goulash. He carefully wiped his mouth so he wouldn't embarrass himself by drooling. He was eager for his portion but waited patiently, knowing he'd be served last. That was the lot of the youngest child. Josip passed him a plate of *Mlinci*, but not before he snagged two slices of the flatbread for himself.

After his plate was heaping with vegetables, rice and goulash, everyone dug in wholeheartedly. *Majka* seemed pleased by the silence, knowing her family was enjoying the meal.

After a few moments, Frank's father wiped the corners of his mouth and said, "How did training go today, Josip?"

"My muscles ache," Josip replied with an exaggerated groan.

The table erupted as Yoshka and Stjepan, Frank's uncles, joined his father as they chorused their understanding of the rigors of training with the local firefighters.

"You'll thank Jakov for those exercises when you're fighting to save a home from a blazing fire," Yoshka said. "It's worth it."

"I know," Josip said with a grin. "It wasn't so bad."

"When can I start training?" Frank asked.

"Soon," Ivan said with a smile as he leaned over and pinched Frank's upper arm. "You need to add a little meat to these bones first."

Frank blushed. "I'm ready now," he murmured.

Josip leaned into him. "It's a lot of work. You have to lug buckets and buckets of water to be poured into the engine. They're heavy."

"When I was younger, we didn't have an engine. We had to form a line and pass water buckets to pour on the fire. It's one thing to lift a bucket and another to keep it steady

CHAPTER TWO

enough not to lose half the contents," Ivan said with a shake of his head.

"When did the fire department get the engine?" Yoshka asked.

"We've had it for a few months, maybe half a year," Ivan replied. "It's so much easier and more effective."

"Remember when we saved the Horvat barn?" Josip said, sitting up straight in his chair.

"We didn't lose a single animal," Ivan said, pride in his voice.

"That was before we came," Stjepan said.

Frank listened to them swap stories of fighting fires with rapt attention. He couldn't wait until he was old enough to join the volunteers just like the rest of the Katana men. Firefighting was in his blood.

Majka put an arm around her son. "Keep working hard on your schoolwork. That's an important job, too."

Ivan winked at him. "I heard you did well on your math today. Division. Never could get the hang of that."

Frank smiled at him. "It's not so hard."

Chapter Three

Summer 1943

Frank leaned on his elbow and toyed with the soft grass as he listened to Habeki, the local brass band. His mother's brother played the trombone in the ten-player band. He loved these lazy summer days. He closed his eyes and allowed the music to flow over him.

"Do you want another sandwich?" he heard his mother ask him.

"No, I'm stuffed," he said, feeling himself drift off to sleep. It was easy to do with the warm sun beating down and the lovely music playing. He lay back on the ground and took a short nap.

It was nearly thirty minutes later that Frank was jostled awake by Jelik. "Come on, sleepy head," he said. "Toma and Leo are starting a football game. We need a goalie."

He jumped up, not needing to be asked twice. He turned back to *Majka*. "Can I go?"

"Sure, sure," she said, waving her arm in their direction. "Get some exercise."

Frank blocked about half the shots, just slightly better than his counterpart on the other team. When they won, Frank cheered loudly and followed his team over to the small table on which stood a large jug of lemonade. He filled his cup and looked around at the growing crowd. So many people attended these events that he didn't even know them all.

CHAPTER THREE

Frank spotted his father taking long strides toward him, an intense and determined expression on his face. Frank's mind raced, trying to figure out what he might have done wrong. He couldn't think of anything, but he found himself trembling nonetheless.

When his father came within earshot, he called out, "Frankie, I have someone I'd like you to meet." As he got closer, Frank noticed he had a twinkle in his eye.

"Really?" Frank said, releasing the pent-up breath he'd been holding, relieved his father wasn't angry. "Who?"

"His name's Drago. Come on, he's over here."

Frank followed his father over to a large tree. Three men were chatting in the shade of its massive sweeping branches.

"Ivan," a tall, thin man with a pencil mustache called out. "Is this the son you were telling me about?"

"That's right," Frank's father said. "He's been talking about becoming a cobbler for a few years now." He turned to Frank and said, "Son, this is Drago. Drago, this is my youngest boy, Frank."

"I hear you have another on the way," one of the other men said. "Congratulations!"

"Yes, Stefanija is praying for a girl," he said with a grin. "I'd like one, too."

"So, Frank," Drago said. "How old are you?"

"I'll be twelve next January," he said, straightening to make himself look taller.

"When will you be finished with grade school?"

"I will be done just before the summer."

"Ho, that's early," Drago said with an approving look.

"Yes, sir. I like studying."

"That's a good thing. What subject do you like best?"

Frank pondered that question. "I like math. And history. And geography. I don't know. I guess I like everything pretty well."

Drago nodded. "What do you think of becoming my apprentice?"

Frank's heart hammered in his chest. He stared into the kind brown eyes of the man in front of him and nodded emphatically. He turned to his father. "May I?"

"I'll need you this fall, but after the new year, I think it would be a good idea," Ivan said.

Drago nodded. "Frank, you'll have to walk each day. I'm not too close. My shop's in Veliki Bukovec."

"I have a bike."

"Even better."

Drago reached out his hand to Frank with a broad grin. Frank took it with pride. "It's a deal then. I'll teach you everything I know, and you'll work hard for me."

"Deal!" Frank said, pumping the man's hand up and down enthusiastically.

* * *

The following year flew by. Frank worked at the farm every evening and got up first thing in the morning to do his chores before he raced to Drago's shop to learn everything he could about repairing and making shoes by hand. When he first started, his fingers were sore and blistered, but soon they adapted to the work, and it became easier.

Frank was not afraid of hard work. Far from it, he liked the feeling that came with being productive. So when the Brcko-Banovici railroad line was being built, Frank eagerly joined this project, knowing what it meant to his country and his people. Many young men and women were recruited, as they were considered pioneering builders of the future who would move the society forward. In the end, the line would be ninety-two kilometers long and would connect the rich coal deposits in Bosnia with various other hubs in Yugoslavia.

CHAPTER THREE

Frank felt proud, toiling shirtless and sweating with his friends in the summer months. He made new friends as well, as the feeling of accomplishment was shared by so many teens that year.

"How many kids do you think are building this thing?" Jelik asked him as he leaned against his shovel.

"Father said it was more than fifty thousand," Frank replied.

"With all that manpower, it'll be built quickly."

Jelik was right. The project was completed ahead of time. Three long tunnels and almost two dozen bridges were a part of this impressive line. Not only did Yugoslavia have a new source of badly needed coal, but the return trip brought food to the starving residents of Bosnia.

On November 7, 1946, Frank and Jelik cheered as news of the first train successfully completing its journey reached their hometown.

"How many railways have been built by children?" Frank's mother asked.

"I've never heard of one," his father said, ruffling Frank's hair affectionately. "I have the feeling that you may have broken some records and made world history."

* * *

When the railway was finished, Frank was invited to join the volunteer fire fighters of Mali Bukovec. No one could say he was still too young. The training was rigorous, but Frank was up to the task.

One evening the family was sitting around the large pine table relaxing after a fine meal of stuffed peppers and sauteed vegetables. There was a hush that came from the contentment of full bellies.

Frank sat up at the sound of footsteps running up the front path. When the front door slammed open, he knew it wasn't good news.

"There's a fire up on the hill," Patrik said. His young round face was etched with worry. "I think it's the Šimić house."

"How many firemen are there?" Ivan asked, shooting out of his chair. Stjepan and Yoshka also stood up and raced over to their shoes by the front door. Josip joined them.

Patrik shook his head. "I don't know. Erik and Adrian went to get the others."

Frank watched them all, stunned, before he suddenly realized he was needed as well. He pushed his brother aside to get to his shoes and coat and followed everyone outside.

"Stay to the back," Frank's father yelled to him as they all ran to the Šimić house. Fortunately, it wasn't very far, but Frank was starting to feel the burn in his legs.

Ivan watched him as they ran. "That's why running is always a part of your training. You never know when or where a fire will flare."

Frank nodded and continued to run past the barn. He made a mental note to run more as his lungs started to struggle. At least he was no longer cold, as the exercise made him want to shed his warm coat.

Finding the Šimić house wasn't a problem, as the blaze lit the night sky. Fear strangled any remaining breath as he wondered about the Šimićs and their children. They had seven kids. Had they all survived? Nikola had been in his class when he'd been in school. Where was he now? Was he all right?

Frank found his second wind and pumped his legs as hard as he could. He knew how fast a fire could ravage a home. They had to get there in time to save it!

When they came up to the property, Frank let out a relieved sigh. "It's just the barn," he cried out.

CHAPTER THREE

"Yes, but if we don't manage the fire, it will spread to the house," Ivan said.

Frank saw that Jakov and four others from the fire department were there with the horse-drawn fire engine. Frank was impressed as he watched the men fill the cylinder with buckets. It was such a bustle; he wasn't sure how to help without getting in the way.

"Come on," Ivan urged as he ran to pick up two remaining buckets. "You help fill."

Frank grabbed the bucket and filled it with water. He ran over to the engine, water slopping over the edge of the bucket.

Ivan shook his head. "You need to move quickly but keep the water in the bucket. Not too quickly, but as fast as you can. Accuracy is more important."

Frank nodded and improved the second time, earning an approving nod from the others. As they continued to work, more and more men came to help. By the time the cylinder of the pump was filled, there were fifteen men on the scene.

Eight of the strongest firefighters, including Frank's father, took positions by two long rods and began pumping as other men took the hose and aimed it at the fire. The men switched places after a few minutes. Frank had tried out the hand pump in training and knew just how difficult it was to rapidly pump it up and down. Even the strongest men needed to switch off.

It was a good thing that there was a well-worn path to the Šimić property, Frank thought. The engine was so much faster than the old bucket brigade, but that would have been needed if the horses hadn't been able to pull the engine up to the site. As it was, the pump worked beautifully, and the fire was extinguished quickly.

The men breathed a collective sigh of relief as the smoke turned white and the last of the flames disappeared.

Frank turned to look at the family. He counted the heads and grinned when he realized they were all there, including his friend. Then he saw the look on Mr. and Mrs. Šimić's faces and realized what the fire had cost them. He turned to his father. "What about their barn?"

Ivan looked at him with sweat pouring down his face. "We'll rebuild it this Sunday. It won't take long. And we'll all contribute some grain and canned vegetables so they can make it through the rest of the winter. Spring's almost here. Somehow they will manage."

Frank nodded and looked at the family he'd helped to save. To say he felt proud would be an understatement. Any tiredness was instantly gone, and he felt as if he were taller than the trees surrounding the Šimić home. He was a Katana firefighter, just like his father and just like Ivan's father before him.

Chapter Four

Summer 1955

Frank's body ached. It had been another long day at the sweltering shoe factory. The old brick building had no ventilation to speak of, and by late morning the heat had become unbearable. His supposed right-hand man, Luka, hadn't shown up until noon and the other assistant, Janko, had fallen asleep in the backroom again, probably hung over from too much cheap red wine from the night before. It was becoming a bad habit.

Fortunately Frank's room wasn't far—only a little over a kilometer away. He preferred to walk, especially on the rare occasions when he got off before dinner. Not only did it give him a chance to stretch his legs and get a little exercise, but he could avoid the crowded *Zagrebački* trams filled with the unappealing smells of unwashed bodies, alcohol, and cigarette smoke.

As he walked along, his stomach growled angrily at him. There'd been no time to eat all day. He'd just managed to snack on a few dried pieces of fish he'd crammed into his pocket when he'd left his place. Who could take time off when they were short two men for half the day? Quotas still had to be met, and he was ultimately responsible.

How he missed the simpler days when he'd come home from school and been greeted by the sweet aromas of his mother's cooking. She had always had something ready for him after school.

And those breakfasts…

Frank stopped in the middle of the sidewalk and nearly groaned. He could smell the sizzling bacon and scrambled eggs, along with the warm rolls right out of the oven. He suddenly felt faint from hunger and wondered if he might have a bit of bread left in his room.

His room.

Frank scoffed. It wasn't really his room. It was just a small bed crammed in next to an old, dilapidated washer and dryer. The machines made a racket every time the owner used them, starting at six in the morning almost every day. Frank preferred the roosters back home. They made more pleasant alarm clocks.

During the summer days, the room became unbearably hot, so he was forced to vacate it on his weekly day off.

It had been four years since Frank had moved to Zagreb. At the time it had made sense, but now he doubted his decision. Maybe farm life wasn't so unbearable, after all. Anything would be better than this life of bare bones survival.

Everyone he knew lived in crowded apartments, often with their extended families. Most people shared rooms, and some even shared beds when needed. He didn't even want to think about the long lines to use the communal bathrooms.

When he'd announced to his mother that he was leaving home to move to the large, bustling city, she'd turned ashen, and tears immediately streamed from her eyes.

"Don't cry," Frank had pleaded.

"I can't bear to be apart from you so long," she'd said.

"I have to try," he said. "I want to see what I can do."

"You've been doing a fine job in Veliki Bukovec. And it's so much closer to home."

CHAPTER FOUR

Frank let out a sigh. "We've been over this. It's a small shop. I've learned everything I'm going to learn from Drago. I need to see what Zagreb can offer me."

She shook her head. "Such big talk for a little boy."

Frank's whole body had shaken with mirth at that. "I think you're the only one to call me little, *Majka*!"

She gave him a feeble smile as she looked up into his eyes. Frank had last measured himself to be one meter eighty-eight. "Why can't you be a farmer like your brother, Josip?"

He knew she knew the answer, so he didn't bother to reply. Instead he just wrapped her in a warm embrace and breathed in her scent of cinnamon and lemon. He cradled her until her sobs lessened.

As he stood there now, in the street in Zagreb, he could still smell that combination of scents that was uniquely *Majka*.

Frank shook himself. No, living the life of a farmer wasn't for him. No matter how hard his life was here in this city, he knew it wouldn't be that way forever. It just couldn't be.

When he got home, he found a few slices of stale bread and a slice of cheese in the communal kitchen. They weren't technically his, but he hoped no one would notice the missing items. Eva, the landlord, never complained when he shaved off a piece of cheese. Frank assumed she knew.

He sighed again. Rent was due the next day. He didn't have it. Eva was often understanding, but last time she'd chided him for a full twenty minutes. It had been pointless to explain that Hinko, the owner of Lovric Shoes, hadn't paid Frank on time. Again. Frank knew that the money most likely went to *Rakija*, Hinko's favorite drink. The scrawny man always smelled of the fruity brandy. This time he could offer her a little more than half of what was due until Hinko paid him. It was the best he could do.

THE SOUL OF A SHOEMAKER

* * *

Frank woke up before Eva came downstairs with the laundry. He pulled out a few bills and put them on his roughly made bed before he left. He hoped Eva would understand that he was doing his best. Frank was sick and tired of living with the restrictions that came with a weak and floundering economy. And if that wasn't bad enough, the government oppressed all opposition to its policies. They never let anyone forget who was in charge. Everywhere Frank turned, he was reminded of the government leadership. Even the street he lived on, Ivo Lola Ribara, was named after a Communist leader and Tito's close friend.

He made himself some coffee and grabbed a slice of bread before he opened the front door. As was his daily routine, he brought in the milk that was sitting on the stoop. Frank helped himself to a glass and relished the cold liquid that satiated his gnawing hunger. Then he sliced off a piece of dried meat and munched on it as he walked to work. The early morning sun glowed on the city that was still sleeping for the most part. It was actually quite pretty this time of the morning.

As he walked down the street, he stepped around a street sweeper who used a large broom made of twigs. Frank enjoyed the sounds of the early morning: the ring of bicycle bells in the distance mixed with the clatter of horse hooves and the jangle of milk cans being delivered. The clanging reminded him of how his father and brother would deliver extra milk to the dairy back home for a few additional coins.

He wasn't the only one who'd migrated from a small village. Each year, Zagreb had grown as more and more people came to make better money in the bustling city. Lots of students also found their way there, as the university was free, and many were eager to take advantage of that.

CHAPTER FOUR

He squinted up at a street sign as he crossed the street and sighed. It bothered him that the old Croatian names for the roads had been replaced with Socialist names. Many streets in Yugoslavia now bore the name of their ruler, Josip Broz Tito. Even the large square in Zagreb had been changed from *Kazališni trg* (Theater Square) to *Trg maršala Tita* (Marshal Tito Square) when the man came into power after World War II. Frank grimaced as he continued to walk down the street. Were they supposed to worship the man? Judging by the number of statues that continued to be erected in his honor, he guessed the answer was yes.

Frank didn't have time to think about politics. It was time to focus on making shoes. As the large gothic cathedral bell rang six o'clock, he opened the double metal doors to the shop, switched on the lights, and started working.

A little over two hours later Bruno and Damir came in. They immediately set to work. Frank looked at the large clock on the wall and wondered what Miss Grzanic would have said about the tardiness of these men. He had to suppress a grin as he wondered what would happen if she tried to paddle them. These tall, bulky men, strong and fit, probably wouldn't submit to her punishments.

When the bells rang out ten times, Hinko stumbled in through the front door. He gave a large yawn that ended with a resounding belch before he walked over to Frank.

"Do you have the orders ready?" he barked.

"Which orders?" Frank responded without thinking.

He immediately realized his error when Hinko's face turned red. "Why the hell should I know? That's what I hired you for!"

Of course he wouldn't know the specifics of the orders. He'd just posed a general question and wanted to know that everything was running smoothly.

Frank nodded. "Everything will be delivered on time by Friday."

"Good," Hinko said and gave another belch. The smell of sour milk wafted over to Frank, and he wondered if his boss ever bathed. The man turned to walk back to the front door.

"Sir?" Frank asked, his voice tentative.

Hinko turned around to face him. "Yeah, boy? What is it?"

"It's about my pay, sir," he said. He winced when he saw Hinko's face turn stormy again. "It's just…you're a few weeks behind and my rent is due."

And my stomach is empty.

"You'll get paid when I get paid. When this order is filled," he growled.

Frank gave him a measured look. That wouldn't fly. He could tell the man was lying to him. He knew enough about business to know that Hinko wouldn't be able to run a company without some money in reserves. There had to be dinars from the last few sales. After all, he had a few large companies that bought wholesale from him on a regular basis.

However, calling his boss a liar probably wouldn't go over well. And it could get him fired. This was a tightrope he had to cross carefully.

Chapter Five

Handled wrong and the man was likely to cuff him. Of course, that would be a mistake on the man's part. Hinko might weigh a few stones more than him, but Frank was all muscle. Still, getting into a brawl with your boss was never a good idea, especially when he owed you money.

Frank relaxed his expression and forced his lips into a small smile. People responded better to smiling faces.

"I'll work hard for you," Frank said, splaying his hands in front of him. "I just need to pay my landlord. I'm overdue and if I get kicked out, I'll need to go home to Mali Bukovec. That's where my folks live. Perhaps I should reconsider farming. It wasn't so bad. Certainly, it was less hours than working in this factory."

Frank paused to see how his words were being received. He'd kept his voice even and light but made sure not to flinch from the man's blood shot eyes. He didn't want to appear to be a threat but wanted Hinko to know that he wasn't about to back down.

Hinko's eyes widened slightly, then they darted around the room.

He's afraid of losing me, Frank thought. *Good*.

As Frank followed Hinko's perusal of the room, he imagined the man was considering how his business would run without Frank. For one thing, he'd need to get up early and open the shop. He'd need to find another manager. When Hinko's bloodshot eyes turned back to Frank's calm ones, he saw a spark of fear, and Frank knew his boss understood how valuable Frank was to him. He wouldn't be able to fill the order without Frank's help.

Frank knew enough to remain silent and allow the man to sort through the options. Frank focused on breathing. Steady breathes in and out. It was important to stay composed and give the appearance of self-confidence. His little speech had been a bluff, but Hinko had no way of knowing that Frank would never go back to farming. No matter how bad it got, at least he wasn't dealing with manure, weeds, milking cows, pecking chickens and all the rest that went with farm life.

The silence seemed to draw out forever before Hinko looked away again. Frank's heart beat a little faster and he knew he'd won. It was one of the oldest games known to man. He who looks away first loses.

"Fine," Hinko said. "I'll get the money to you by the end of the day."

"All of it?" Frank asked, feeling braver.

"Yes." With that, Hinko turned and stormed away.

Frank's eyes followed him out the door before he continued to assemble a pair of men's formal shoes. He sincerely hoped that Luka would arrive soon. He really needed the man's help. Besides, the young man wasn't bad company. Frank just wished he'd show up on time more often than he did. Hinko never seemed to notice, so Luka's job wasn't in jeopardy.

Frank was Janko's and Luka's manager, but he didn't have the heart to chew them out or even to correct them. It seemed disloyal somehow. After all, they were his friends. He liked the extra coin that management brought; that is, when Hinko could be convinced to actually pay him. However, Frank didn't enjoy ordering people around.

Frank hadn't much liked the army when he'd served his mandatory eighteen-month stint. He'd kept his head down and just did what he was told. He never tried for advancement. He'd preferred taking orders to issuing them.

However, if he wanted to make good money, he knew he'd have to take charge eventually. Being a broke laborer wasn't what he wanted. He sat back in his chair and wondered what it would be like to own this shop. What could he accomplish with it? Without the deadweight of Hinko and the others, he was sure he could turn a better profit than Hinko.

Could he, though?

Living in Zagreb, he wasn't sure anyone could do much better. That's probably why Hinko was always drinking. Thinking it over, Frank realized he didn't know anyone who was wealthy. Well, maybe his first landlord.

What a nightmare he had been.

Old Mr. Sever. He'd been in his late eighties and was the stingiest man he'd ever met, except when it came to alcohol. The man had dinars, that was for sure. He'd been a furrier by trade in his youth and had done well. One thing Mr. Sever knew how to do was hoard cash. Frank always wondered where—probably under his large, ornate bed.

Mr. Sever started drinking when the sun came up. Every morning he drank slivovitz, ate garlic kielbasa, and didn't stop until he passed out at night, usually in his clothes. Frank had tried that plum brandy once, thinking it couldn't be very potent because it was as clear as water. Boy, had he been surprised. He'd nearly spit it out, making Mr. Sever laugh so hard he almost coughed up his breakfast.

Frank eventually had to leave. That apartment was too expensive for him and, to save money, Mr. Sever often refused to turn on the hot water; so he almost froze to death every time he took a shower. In the end, Frank had developed some god-awful illness like bronchitis and had coughed up blood for a month.

It had been such a relief when Frank had found the place with Eve. Yes, it was small and cramped, but it cost about half as much as other places. At least he could afford it, and the shower was nice and hot.

He'd earned his cobbler's master's diploma back in Ludbreg when he was seventeen. That should have opened more doors for him, but he found that the shop keepers weren't paying much more for skilled labor.

Other countries are different. I'm sure of it.

He'd heard a few people talk about Australia in hushed tones one day at Mr. Sever's home. It was clear they were making plans to go there.

Mr. Sever had known all kinds of people. That was one of the good things about living in that home. Since he'd been so successful as a furrier, he'd made a lot of connections. Although he was stingy with most things, people knew he'd open a new bottle of slivovitz when they came over. He liked to keep the glasses full. Although he didn't mind drinking alone, he seemed to prefer getting drunk with company.

Frank would crack the door to his room open so he could listen to them talk. It was always fascinating. Sometimes he'd learn a thing or two about business and making money before they were all too sloshed to speak coherently.

"How you goin' to get all the way there? Swim?" Mr. Sever had said when his guests told him about their plans to leave Yugoslavia and move to Australia.

Australia?

Frank had tiptoed over to the door to peek out. There were two men sitting with Mr. Sever. Both guffawed for a few minutes at his quip, which probably wouldn't have been as funny had he not just splashed another glass full of plum brandy for them.

"Haven't figured out how yet," the thin, wiry man with a goatee said.

CHAPTER FIVE

"Careful," the other man had said in a hushed voice. He'd tugged on his well-worn fedora, then said. "Walls can have ears, you know."

Mr. Sever waved his hand impatiently. "Not these walls." Just then his eyes swiveled over to land on Frank.

Frank quickly ducked back into the shadows, his heart hammering in his chest. He prayed the man hadn't seen him. After all, it was a treasonous conversation they were having.

Mr. Sever shook his head and cleared his throat. "These walls have better things to do than report a discussion to the government officials," he said in a loud voice. "Isn't that right Frank Katana?"

Frank's ears were filled with the sound of rushing blood. "Yes, sir," his shaky voice replied.

"Come in here, boy," Mr. Sever said. "Come in and meet my friends."

Frank took a tentative step through his door and leaned against the wall of the common room. The two other men gave him a wary look, and Frank decided to study the pattern of the maroon area rug that covered the floor. Mr. Sever had picked it up from some people visiting from Turkey. It was hand-knotted, something Mr. Sever bragged about to anyone who would listen.

"This is Zoran and Mirko," said Mr. Sever. "And this is my boarder, Frank. He's a good boy. You don't have to worry."

"What is it that you do?" Zoran asked, removing his hat to scratch his head. "You're a furrier like Gordan here?"

Gordan. So that's his first name. Frank had only known him as Mr. Sever.

"No, sir. I'm a cobbler," Frank replied.

"That's not a bad trade," Zoran said. "Make good money?"

Frank shook his head. "Not really. But I get by." He glanced at Mr. Sever to see if he was listening but saw that the man was busy chugging down a glass of brandy. He sighed. "I hope to have my own shop one day."

Mirko shook his head. "Won't do you much good," he said. "It's hard to make much money here when no one has dinars to spend."

"So you think Australia's better?" Frank whispered. While Mr. Sever's house stood on its own and didn't share any walls with neighbors, he still didn't want to take the chance that someone might overhear his words and land him in prison for the rest of his life.

The two men nodded their heads vigorously in unison.

"*Apsolutno!*" Zoran said. "No doubt."

"The sky's the limit, as they say in America," Mirko said.

"That's another place to consider," Mr. Sever said.

"Yeah," Zoran said. "But I know a few people in Australia. That's why we're going there."

Frank was torn. He had so many questions but knew that every moment he participated in this conversation, they all risked being caught somehow. However, he was behind closed doors, so the danger seemed minimal. Still his heart hammered loudly in his chest as he asked, "How will you cross the border?"

The three fell silent and Frank knew at that moment they felt just as nervous as he did. Finally Zoran cleared his throat and said, "We'll cross the way everyone else does. By train, then by foot into Austria. That's really the only way."

Frank nodded. "But where?"

"Why do you want to know, kid?" Mirko asked gruffly. "You thinking of defecting, too?"

Frank shook his head. "No. Just curious. I wondered how it was done."

Mirko shrugged. "We'll go north, up through Maribor. Then we'll get off before the last stop."

CHAPTER FIVE

Frank nodded. "Sounds good." It was one of those pieces of information he knew he'd probably never need, but still, he was glad he'd asked.

The conversation continued on into the wee hours. Frank slipped away when the talk turned to girls. He had to get up early and didn't have an interest in their lewd discussion.

Frank snapped himself out of his daydream and began sewing the shoe in front of him again.

Australia. Now that was a place that had promise. Frank never found out what happened to Zoran and Mirko, but he always imagined they made it and were thriving in the foreign country. More and more he found himself wishing he had the nerve to try to escape; complete freedom sounded good.

Chapter Six

Frank could count the number of decent friends he had on one hand and Luka was on top of that list. When the end of summer came, Luka announced that he was moving away. Frank was sad to see him go, but Luka was adamant.

"I can't afford to live here anymore," he said, running his hand through his dark curly hair. "I can't make enough to even eat two meals a day."

"Where will you go?" Frank asked.

"I have a cousin in Maribor. His name is Petar and he said I could live with him. Cost of living is much better."

Frank nodded. "When do you go?"

"Two weeks."

"Before you leave, let's go to a concert together. I'm going this weekend to visit my folks in Mali Bukovec. Come with me. We'll have fun."

Luka grinned. "Count me in."

Frank was able to take a couple days off from work, and they took the train back to Frank's home. His mother cried when she saw him coming up the road, and she instantly fed him full of cabbage rolls and *Mlinci*. It was as if no time had passed.

"This is delicious," Luka said in wonder.

Frank smiled as he watched his friend's eyes close in pleasure. "I missed this," Frank had to admit.

The next day, the family got up early and everyone made short work of the farm chores. Luka was happy to lend a hand.

CHAPTER SIX

"I could see doing this for a living," Luka said to Frank. "What made you give it up?"

Frank rolled his eyes at his friend. "It's fine for one day, but stepping in *sranje* all day isn't my idea of living the high life."

* * *

It was late morning when the family set off for the large park and laid out their blankets under a large tree close to where the band would be. They had brought along three picnic baskets filled to the rim with goodies, which *Majka* laid out as soon as they arrived.

"Best get them before the ants do!" she said.

Frank and Luka dug in as they settled down to watch the brass band set up. It was a large twelve-piece ensemble. As they got organized, Frank noticed a pretty girl laughing with the tuba player, and he instantly felt jealous. He shook his head and laughed to himself, wondering at that odd emotion.

The girl wore a dull brown sleeveless dress over a pristine white pressed cotton shirt. Her long black hair was pulled back in a chignon, and Frank found himself wondering what it would look like falling loose around her shoulders.

"She's so pretty," Frank said low under his breath.

"Who?" Luka said as he munched on *sarma*, cabbage stuffed with sausage, and *strukli*, pastry stuffed with cottage cheese.

Frank glanced over at him in disbelief. How could his friend not be looking at the glorious angel only twenty meters in front of them? "The girl. Over there," he said, resuming his adoration of her.

"It looks like she has a boyfriend," Luka said with a shrug.

Frank shook his head. "You don't know that."

Just then the band began to tune up, and the girl took a seat on the grass with what looked like her family. Frank waited until the music started and various couples began to dance before he popped up and walked over to her.

When he arrived, she was chatting with a younger girl. He waited for the vision in brown to look up. This gave him a chance to study her delicate features and creamy, flawless skin. When she looked up at him, his heart stopped for a moment at those intelligent brown eyes with small gold flecks. He held out his hand and said, "My name is Frank. What is your name?"

She blushed. "Ljubica," she replied. "Ljubica Kermek."

"What a beautiful name!" he exclaimed. "I do believe it means love and violets, does it not?"

She nodded and blushed deeper, which Frank found enchanting. "Yes."

"May I have this dance?" he asked.

She just stared at him for a moment, then slowly shook her head. "No."

He nodded but didn't feel put off in the slightest. There was something in her eyes that told him she'd eventually say yes. So he bowed majestically and left, offering her a small smile.

When he came back to Luka empty-handed, his friend grinned at Frank. "Didn't get the girl, I see."

"No," Frank replied. "But I will."

He couldn't take his eyes off the girl. When she got up to walk around the park, he followed her and asked again if she might dance with him. "Just once," he said with what he hoped was a charming smile. He'd been told his smile was one of his best features.

"I don't know," she said, looking down at her hands.

"What brings you to Mali Bukovec?" he asked. "I've never seen you here before."

"I'm visiting my uncle and cousins," she said, looking back up at him.

"Oh? And where do you live?"

"At the Maruševec castle. The orphanage," she replied.

Frank nodded. They sat down under a tree and Ljubica shared with him how she'd lost her parents shortly after World War II, when she was eight. She had five siblings. The two youngest lived with their grandmother, but since she couldn't take all six, the other four had to live in orphanages scattered around the country.

Frank's heart went out to her. His house had always been crowded, and he couldn't imagine what his childhood would have been like without his family around him.

"You've been through so much," he said.

Ljubica shrugged. "It's not so much. The orphanage is strict, but I get along with the other girls, and the directors are nice. It's hard work, but I don't mind."

"How old are you?" Frank suddenly wondered at her maturity.

"I'm sixteen," she said shyly. "How old are you?"

He grinned. It was the first question she had had for him. He liked that she was curious about him as well. "I'm twenty-three," he replied.

"What do you do?"

He gave her a warm smile. "I'm a master cobbler. I work in Zagreb. I've been in the trade ever since I left school when I was twelve."

Ljubica's eyes shown with admiration. "That's over ten years."

"That's right. One day I'll own my own business."

They fell silent. Then Frank asked. "How often do you get to visit your family?"

"Some weekends. I usually see my grandmother or my aunts and uncles. But I always work hard wherever I go. They need help with the farm, and I am invited so I can help out with the chores."

"Well, I'm glad you could come out and see this concert today!" Frank said.

"My cousin Joska is the tuba player," she said. "We wanted to see him play."

Frank felt joy course through his body, and he grinned at her. "Ah, that was the man you were talking to," he said.

"Yes," she said, looking a little confused by his reaction. "He's good, isn't he?"

"The best!" Frank cried, standing up. "Come now, let's not waste the afternoon sitting here. Come dance with me." He reached out a hand and this time Ljubica didn't hesitate but accepted it, much to his pleasure.

Frank pulled her along and brought her to the dance area, where they danced the next three dances in a row. She felt so right in his arms, and Ljubica seemed to enjoy their closeness as much as he did. He reluctantly let her return to her family after the third song because he didn't want to appear overbearing. But the following hours crawled by as he sat, looking forlorn, next to Luka, who teased him mercilessly.

By the time the band played their last song of the day, most of the people on the grass had left. Ljubica's family was packing up as Frank approached her.

"I hope to see you again!" he said.

She blushed and smiled but didn't say anything. Again there was something in her eyes that told Frank he wasn't alone in his feelings. There was a mutual attraction. But she was young, and he still needed to prove himself to her.

One day.

Yes, one day he'd find a way to give her the life she deserved.

Chapter Seven

Summer turned into fall, which turned into winter and back into spring. Frank continued to work for Hinko at Lovric Shoes. Nothing seemed to improve. In fact, supplies were harder to get than ever before. There were always delays on much-needed leather and other supplies, which put Hinko into a perpetually bad mood and pushed him to drink even more.

The first month after the concert, Frank missed Luka, so he'd take the train up to visit him whenever he could. Petar, Luka's cousin and roommate, had become his friend as well. They'd often invite a neighbor over for a rousing game of *Šuster* and play into the wee hours of the night. Frank rarely won as there were only so many sevens in the deck and they never seemed to fall into his hand. However, he didn't mind, as he always had fun.

Hinko had been reluctant to hire another employee to replace Luka, but he did. Unfortunately, it was Hinko's cousin who had recently moved to Zagreb. The kid was much worse than Luka had been. He showed up on time but was useless when it came to hand sewing shoes. Frank found he had to redo half of his orders.

Frustrated, Frank looked for another job but quickly discovered that no one was hiring. So he continued to put up with Hinko. Eva had raised his rent, which meant Frank had even less money for food. That, and the severe shortages that always seemed to crop up, was making life more and more unbearable.

One evening when Frank was on his way home, late as usual, he stopped before he reached his door. Across the street, three uniformed men were taking boxes out from one of the apartments. There was only one reason that could happen. Someone had tried to escape across the border and was now in prison for his efforts. Probably for at least five years. All the poor man's belongings would be pawed through by the local police and confiscated by the state.

Frank ducked his head and walked through the front door.

"Have my rent?" Eva said by way of greeting.

He studied the slight, elderly woman. He couldn't fault her. She needed to eat as well, and the price of milk and meat had gone up again. And the coal her little stove required cost more than it had last month. Evenings were still chilly.

Frank sighed. "I'll try to get it to you by the end of the week," he said. "That's the best I can do."

"That boss of yours needs to pay you," she muttered.

Frank knew she would have a difficult time renting out the bed in the laundry room. Not many people would put up with that kind of accommodation. But then again, that's probably why she never mentioned how her cheese was a little thinner after he'd been in the kitchen.

She must know.

Frank gave her a small smile. "I'll make sure he does."

Just then a knock sounded at the front door, and Frank turned to open it. There was Mrs. Budimir, a stout woman with a permanent scowl on her face. She pushed past Frank and stood in front of Eva.

"Did you hear about Vlado?" she asked in a stage whisper.

"No," Eva replied.

"He was carted off to Goli Otok," she said. Frank was disgusted. This toad of a woman actually looked happy about the appalling news.

CHAPTER SEVEN

Goli Otok was a nasty island prison filled with people who had tried to flee Yugoslavia or who'd said an unkind word about President Tito. Frank had heard stories of the horrid conditions at that place. No matter the weather, each inmate was expected to slave in the stone quarry. In the winter many died from the freezing winds, while in the summer heat stroke was common as the temperatures rose into the forties.

Frank's heart went out to the people there. "That's awful," Frank murmured.

Mrs. Budimir gave him a pinched look. "What do you mean?"

"I mean that place is evil," he said. "It's inhuman."

"You're not saying that he didn't deserve what he got. Are you?"

Frank furrowed his brows. "No one deserves that."

The woman gasped. "No one? Not even those who betray our fatherland?"

"It's cruel," Frank protested.

"So is speaking out against our great leader," she snapped back.

"Don't you think we should have the right to say what we think? In the privacy of our homes? Without fear of imprisonment?"

Mrs. Budimir gasped again, this time more dramatically.

Eva gave Frank a slight shake of her head as he opened his mouth to say something. Frank took the warning, closed his mouth, and said no more.

Eva then turned to her friend. "He doesn't mean anything by it. Come now, Ana. Join me for some coffee."

Mrs. Budimir paused a moment, then gave her friend a curt nod and followed her into the kitchen.

Frank frowned as he watched her leave. How could anyone not think that island prison was horrible? It was. There was no doubt about that. However, she'd looked at him as if he'd said something traitorous. His blood ran cold as he realized that she could report him for what he said.

Would she?

He retraced his words. He hadn't said anything bad about the government, just the prison. Maybe he should go into the kitchen and clarify what he meant. No, it was fine. Better leave it.

* * *

Two days later, Frank was sitting at his workbench wrestling with a particularly stubborn sole, when two uniformed officers walked through the front door. There was no doubt what their purpose was. Frank knew Mrs. Budimir had reported him on suspicion of treason.

As the two officers approached him, Frank replayed the conversation and reviewed his words. He could always deny he had said anything at all, but that probably wouldn't be accepted. No, it was probably best to go with the truth and hope these two officers of the state were reasonable.

The slender man with a neatly trimmed beard and wire-rimmed glasses cleared his throat and said, "Mr. Frank Katana?"

"Y-yes?" Frank responded, hating how his voice quivered. Would that make him sound more guilty?

The second officer, a large brute of a man with a crew cut remained silent and just stared at Frank. Although Frank knew the man was trying to intimidate him, he also knew it was working. Frank could feel beads of sweat forming on his brow.

"I'm Officer Erceg," the slender man said. "And this is Officer Turkalj. Would you come with us, please?"

It was posed as a question, but Frank knew that he had no options. He wasn't free to decline. He nodded and stood up.

CHAPTER SEVEN

Spots blocked his vision and he felt as if the room was reeling. He paused and leaned heavily on his desk for a moment.

"You OK?" Erceg asked.

The man's voice sounded far away and tinny as Frank struggled to not lose consciousness. The last thing he wanted to do was faint in front of his subordinates and these officers.

"Yeah," Frank lied. "Just give me a second."

He struggled to regain his composure. When the spots began to dissipate, he shook his head, straightened, and followed the officers out the front door. He looked around the shop and wondered if he'd be coming back. It wasn't uncommon to go in for questioning and never return.

* * *

Frank shifted in the chair in the small room with no window and one door. Peeling gray paint was the only adornment of the walls and a single lightbulb hung over the steel table in front of him. The hard wooden seat was proving to be horribly uncomfortable after the third hour of interrogation.

Officer Erceg sat across from him, asking the same questions over and over. Frank was pretty sure he'd answered the same each time, but now his mind had turned to mush, and he wasn't sure.

"How do you feel about our president?" Erceg asked.

Frank's eyes flickered over to Officer Turkalj, who still hadn't spoken. Instead, he chose to lean against the back wall with his arms folded across his chest, scowling at him.

Frank wasn't sure if it was his exhaustion or the shards of terror running through his body, but it seemed to him that Turkalj hadn't blinked once during the last three hours. At least if he had, Frank certainly hadn't seen it.

"President Tito is a fine leader," Frank repeated. "I've never said anything bad about him."

"Didn't you?" Erceg said.

"No," Frank said shaking his head. "I think my words were misunderstood."

"And what were your words, again?"

Frank shifted in his chair. "Can I get some water?"

Erceg glanced at Turkalj, who gave a small shake of his head. Erceg turned back to Frank. "No, just answer the question."

"I had told Mrs. Budimir that I thought Goli Otok was awful," he said.

Turkalj cleared his throat. Erceg gave Frank a slight frown, "That's not what Mrs. Budimir said you said." Erceg glanced through the small, frayed notebook he had in front of him, which was filled with notes he continued to take. "She said you said it was *inhuman*."

"Yes, that's right," Frank said.

"Inhuman and awful aren't the same," Erceg said.

"All right."

"They're very different."

"Yes."

"Well then," Turkalj said, as he pushed off from the wall to walk over to the table. He leaned down on both hands and stared at Frank. "Which is it? Inhuman or awful."

Frank gulped. He was no longer sure how he felt. He just prayed he could get out of there. "A-awful?"

"Is that a question or a statement?" Turkalj said with a sneer. He looked back at his partner. "It sounded like a question to me."

Frank looked from one man to the other and exhaled sharply. He could no longer remember much about that evening, but he did know he had called the prison inhuman. When he looked Erceg in the eye, he wondered if the man might have some sympathy for him. He wasn't sure, but he sensed it was possible.

CHAPTER SEVEN

"I...," Frank began. "I said inhuman that night."

"And do you still feel that way?" Erceg prompted.

The man was giving him an out.

"No, sir, I don't," Frank answered in a rush. "I misspoke that evening."

"So you don't think our president is inhuman?" Erceg said.

"No, no," Frank said in a rush. "I *never* said that! I just meant the prison..." he allowed his voice to trail off as he considered his words carefully. He closed his eyes, then opened them to look at Erceg. "The prison *shouldn't* be a nice place. And President Tito has every right to punish people who are traitors to our country."

He let his words hang in the air and hoped they were enough to save him. Turkalj continued to stare at him for a few moments, then gave Erceg a terse nod and walked out the door.

Frank's heart hammered in his chest. What did that mean? Was he going to be allowed to go home, or had he just received a death sentence?

"You're free to go," Erceg said. "Just remember to choose your words more carefully next time."

Frank's body collapsed onto the table in relief. "I will!" he promised. "I will."

Chapter Eight

Frank leaned back on Luka's beige couch, which had so many stains on it he wasn't sure if beige was its original color. It had been a crowded three-hour train ride and he was happy to be at his friend's apartment in Maribor. Although he was struggling to keep his eyes open, having put in a long day at the shop, he was reluctant to call it an evening. He only had one day off a week. That wasn't the time to sleep. No, it was better to make the most of his little vacation, if you could call it that.

He opened his eyes and looked over at Luka and Petar, who were engaged in a discussion about their jobs at the textile factory. They also worked long hours, but neither had a role of responsibility. They both seemed to prefer it that way because they could sometimes slip out and take a nap or goof off when the manager wasn't looking.

"Still getting to work late?" Frank said, his head lolling back against the cushions.

"No," Luka sighed. "The new manager put a stop to that."

"I didn't like it when you did that either, you know," Frank said. "I just put up with it."

Petar groaned. "Antun doesn't put up with it. He doesn't put up with much."

"No," Luka agreed. "But he's not always there watching. That's something."

They sounded as tired as he felt. Frank looked at them both and said, "I wish…" He stopped because there was no point in continuing. He could wish all he liked. It didn't do any good.

However, it seemed logical that if he never allowed himself the luxury of dreaming, he would never be able to change his situation in life. Everything would just stay the same. By wishing, he could perhaps rise above all of this and make a decent living.

"Yes?" Luka asked when he stopped mid-sentence.

Frank sat up. He looked at his friend earnestly and leaned forward. He kept his voice low. "I wish I could sincerely try to make it. You know? Really try to earn what I think I'd be capable of earning. I want to be paid according to my skill and..." he paused and thought about it, "my skill and hard work. I wish working hard mattered."

Frank didn't mind the hard work. The truth was, he liked making and repairing shoes. He knew he was good at it. It was just the measly pay that made life difficult. That, and no hope for improvement.

"You do work hard," Luka said. "I mean, I think I work hard until I look at you. You definitely have us all beat. It would be nice if I could make a little more money. I'm not greedy, but I'd like to be able to afford decent food and a better living space. But no one I know gets paid more. We're all paid the same."

Frank considered his next words carefully, then said, "Not everyone gets paid the same."

Petar scrunched his face in confusion. "What do you mean?"

"I mean, not everyone in the world is paid such low wages as here. Not everyone in the world has to constantly deal with expired food and never-ending shortages," Frank said quietly. He glanced around to make sure there was no one nearby that might overhear him.

His fears were silly, of course, as Luka and Petar didn't share their place with anyone, but the walls were thin. Very thin. He shook his head. They were sitting in the living room, buffered by an exterior wall to the right and a bedroom to the left. It was safe. It should be, but it still didn't feel secure.

"Are you saying what I think you're saying?" Petar asked, his voice equally hushed.

Frank shrugged. "That depends. What do you think I'm saying?"

After his ordeal with the Zagreb police, he wasn't quite sure he could trust Petar. He felt comfortable with Luka and knew his good friend wouldn't turn him in, but he'd only met the cousin on a handful of occasions. Although he considered Petar a friend, he didn't know the young man well. It was tough to trust anyone.

What a sad world they lived in.

Petar and Frank locked eyes for a few moments before Luka said softly, "Don't be like that, Cousin. You might as well tell Frank. He won't turn us in."

Frank felt a lightness in his chest that came with a feeling of hope. Could it be? "Tell me what?" he whispered.

Luka looked at Petar until his cousin gave him a small nod. Then he turned to Frank and said, "We're thinking of leaving. You know, crossing the border."

"Into Austria?" Frank said excitedly. He could feel his heart hammering fiercely in his chest and wondered if the two men across from him could hear it, too. "When?"

"First," Luka said, "are you in? Do you want to come with us?"

The truth was, Frank had been thinking about crossing the border ever since he left the police station three months prior. Not only was he tired of living in poverty, but now he worried about every word that came out of his mouth. Anything, really anything he said might be misconstrued. If

CHAPTER EIGHT

he was hauled in again, he knew there would be no second chances offered. It would be straight to Goli Otok.

After a moment's pause, he said, "*Apsolutno!*"

Petar still looked nervous, which gave Frank more courage. He decided to confide in them both about his recent experience with Officers Erceg and Turkalj. As Frank relayed the story, Petar relaxed more and more.

"You're lucky," Luka said. "You know that, right?"

Frank nodded. "But I didn't even *say* anything. Not really. It was crazy. If I'd said what I actually thought..." He shuddered as he considered what he might have said instead. "So, what's the plan? When do you leave?"

Luka and Petar exchanged looks. "We haven't gotten that far."

Then Luka stood up and walked over to the bedroom. Frank followed him with his eyes, wondering what he'd come back with. He and Petar waited in silence for him to return. Moments later Luka returned with a folded piece of paper. He handed it to Frank.

Frank opened it carefully and found it was a map. It showed details about the border that Frank had never seen. He could see the path across the border wound through forests and farmland.

"Where did you get this?" Frank asked in wonder. "It's great!"

"A friend," Luka said with a shrug. "We know a few guys who left last year. They went to Australia. Sounds like a great place. That's where Petar and I will be headed. Eventually."

Frank nodded. "Yes, I've heard Australia is wonderful." His mind went back to the time he overhead the conversation in Mr. Sever's home. "So, that's where you plan to live. Interesting!"

"Yeah," Luka said. "We'll look up our friends and see where they ended up. They planned to settle just outside of Perth.

I received one letter when they crossed the border, so I know they made it. If they made it across the border, we can, too."

"We should leave while the weather's still nice," Frank said, feeling more and more excited. "It will be harder in the winter."

Petar nodded. "Maybe next month? It would give us a little time to get things in order."

Luka looked at him. "What things?"

Petar shrugged. He appeared to think it over, then said, "I guess I don't have anything here."

"Right," Luka said. "That's the point. If we're going to do this, we should just go."

Suddenly, Frank felt a little short of breath. Things were moving so quickly. It had somehow gone from a fantasy to an imminent reality in the space of a few moments. Was he actually ready to flee? Could he abandon everything and everyone he knew?

He thought of his mother and knew his leaving would break her heart. Would she ever forgive him? What of his sister, Mila, and brother, Josip? They would be devastated, too.

He went cold as he thought about his father. He groaned and leaned back. How could he desert him?

"What is it?" Luka asked, his voice laced with concern.

"It's just my father," Frank said, opening his eyes to look at his friend. "He's got cancer, you know. I'm not sure how long he has to live."

"Oh, that's right," Luka breathed. "He's at the hospital near you. You visit him a lot?"

"Yeah," Frank said. "It's one of the perks of being in Zagreb. I see him every week."

"Do the doctors think they can do anything for him?"

"No. He's got mandibular cancer. It's in his jaw. It's pretty advanced."

CHAPTER EIGHT

Everyone was silent. The doctors had told Frank on his last visit that his father had taken a turn for the worse and that he probably wouldn't live past the winter. They were just trying to keep him comfortable at this point.

Frank sighed. "I wouldn't be able to be there when he passes. I'd miss his funeral."

Luka exhaled long and hard. "That's rough."

"Yeah," Frank said.

"So," Petar said, "do you still want to come?"

Frank nodded. "I can't stay here. Not with the way things are. It's just not safe. And things are getting worse."

"They are. I haven't eaten meat in two weeks. And when was the last time you saw a plum?"

"It's been a while," Frank agreed. The list of things he had to do without kept growing month after month. Toilet paper was often at a premium, so they'd all learned to use as little as possible. He wondered what life would be like in a country you could eat a few plums in one sitting or eat all the meat you could stomach.

"So it's agreed?" Petar said. "We leave as soon as possible. Do you think you can be ready in two weeks?"

Frank nodded. His heart felt heavy at the thought of leaving his family. "That will give me time to say good-bye to Mom and Dad," he murmured.

Luka and Petar jumped off the couch in unison. "No, no!" they cried out. "You can't do that. It could put us all in jeopardy."

"W-what?" Frank asked, suddenly paralyzed with fear. "What do you mean?"

"If you tell them," Luka said, speaking slowly as if talking to a young child, "if you tell *anyone*, they could tell someone else. And then we'd *all* be dead."

Frank shook his head and laughed. "My parents wouldn't say anything!"

"Of course not," Luka replied. "Not intentionally. But you never know. Maybe your mom says something to Josip and a neighbor overhears. Or she tells a friend she trusts, and that friend decides it is her moral obligation to report it."

Frank stared at Luka. His friend was right. The risk was far too great.

"So I just have to leave without saying good-bye?" The words came out in a hoarse whisper. "That's…"

"Horrible, I know," Luka said. "But there's no way around it. The alternative is too dangerous."

Frank nodded woodenly. "All right."

Luka walked over and put a comforting hand on his shoulder. "Come on, let's get some sleep. We'll talk more about it in the morning."

Frank had been looking forward to sleeping in the next day. It was a rare luxury since usually he was woken up at the crack of dawn by Eva's loud washing machine and had his early duties at the shop. However, he found he could hardly sleep that night, what with all the thoughts and plans whizzing around his mind. When morning came, he was tired of lying on the uncomfortable couch. He got up and freshened up in the bathroom. When he came back out, he saw Luka making coffee on the stove.

"Want some?" he asked.

"Desperately." Frank's eyes felt like sandpaper, and he wondered if he'd get even a single good night's sleep in the next two weeks.

Luka laughed. "I feel like you look."

Luka and Frank went out after breakfast and stayed out until midafternoon. They walked all over the city. Frank had the distinct impression they were saying good-bye to all the landmarks.

They stopped in front of a fruit stand in the old square, *Glavni Trg*. A little old woman with a bright green shawl was

CHAPTER EIGHT

hunched over a display of sour cherries. She was doing her best to arrange them in a pleasing presentation despite her crooked fingers, which seemed to pain her.

Frank counted his coins to see if he had enough to purchase a plum and still buy a train ticket back to Zagreb when Luka said, "I'm going to miss this. I doubt Australia has historic structures like this. It's such a new country."

Frank froze and locked eyes with the market woman. She immediately looked down and Frank could see her hands tremble. She hesitated in her task, then continued. It was clear that she'd heard Luka's comment.

Chapter Nine

Frank pulled Luka away by the arm until he was sure they were out of range of any prying ears. "What are you thinking?" he whispered.

Luka looked perplexed by Frank's vehemence. He shook off Frank's grip and asked, "What do you mean?"

Frank leaned close to his friend and whispered in his ear, "You just mentioned *Australia*."

Luka paled. "Oh my God! I-I'm sorry. Do you think she heard?"

"Yes. The question is, will she do anything?"

Luka closed his eyes in frustration. "I'm an idiot," he moaned.

"Wait here," Frank said and walked back over to the woman and bought some cherries. He had calculated he had just enough money to make the purchase and give her a little tip.

"Thank you," she said, looking him in the eye. "You have a good day."

He nodded. "You, too."

She gave him a little smile. Frank knew that he'd probably bought them a little time, but the danger of being caught still loomed over them.

"Look," he said as soon as they got back to Luka's apartment. "It's clear we need to leave soon. I know I can't say good-bye to anyone, but I do want to visit *Majka* one last time. You understand?"

CHAPTER NINE

"Yeah, I plan to spend as much time as possible with my brothers and sisters before we go, too," Luka said. His parents had died a few years ago and all his siblings lived in Maribor, so he wouldn't have far to travel.

"I also want to spend time with my father," Frank said. "I'll see if I can visit him every day."

Luka shook his head slowly. "You can't do anything that would draw attention to our plans. See him twice this week but no more."

Frank's shoulders drooped as he realized his friend was right. It would seem suspicious if he visited more often, especially when he failed to show up the following day.

"You're right."

* * *

Frank approached the large concrete building, his stomach tied up in knots. Although his father rarely talked these days, Frank worried he'd see right through him. After all, they'd always been close.

He passed the reception desk of the hospital and waved to the plump nurse who was on duty. Emilija always had a kind smile for him. She returned his wave. Frank glanced at his watch. In another two and a half hours her shift would be over, and Rosa would take over. Rosa was a little more conservative, but pleasant. He'd miss the staff here.

As he walked down the long corridor to the nurse's station, he took a few deep breaths. This wasn't going to be easy.

He smiled at Vesna and asked, "How is he?" It was more of a ritual than a desire for information. The answer never varied.

"He's the same," she replied. "He'll be happy to see you."

Frank smiled and felt a cold chill as he realized once again that this would be his last visit. For the tenth time that day he wondered if he should leave so soon. Maybe they could wait a few months?

No. We can't.

In a few months the weather would turn cold, which would make their plans for escape much more difficult. It was now or never. He knew that in his heart.

He peeked into his father's room and tiptoed inside. Ivan's head lolled to the left and Frank felt his heart leap into his chest.

Frank chided himself for his fears. His father was just asleep. He hadn't passed. It wasn't his time. However, despite his attempts to reassure himself, he held his breath as he looked for the rhythmic rise and fall of his father's chest. When he saw Ivan exhale, Frank's shoulders relaxed. He took his usual place in the chair by the bed.

He didn't have the heart to wake his father, so he simply put his hand over Ivan's frail one and looked at his slumbering father's face. The mandibular cancer had taken its toll on his father's once-handsome face. It looked ravaged from the war the cancer had waged on his body.

Twenty minutes later, Ivan's eyes fluttered open, and he smiled. "What a lovely surprise," he said.

Frank's lips trembled into a smile. "How are you feeling?"

"Good."

Frank knew it was a lie, but he accepted the answer anyway. "That's good."

Ivan struggled to sit up. Frank stood and helped him get more comfortable. "Better?" he asked.

"Yes. Thank you. How is work?"

"Same. Busy." Again a chill crept up Frank's spine as he wondered how Hinko would react when his best worker failed to show up one day. He'd call in sick just before he boarded the train. That would buy him one day. He could just imagine the look on his boss' face when he realized that Frank would never return.

"Everything all right?" Ivan asked as he studied his son.

Frank shook himself from his thoughts and forced his face to look calm. He put on a bright smile. "Of course, Father. Of course."

They talked about all manner of things, ranging from life in the city through problems at work to reports from Mali Bukovec.

"Your mother is well?"

Frank nodded. "She is in good health, as are all the others. The farm is doing very well. In fact, there are fifty percent more sugar beets by the last count. Mother is very pleased."

Ivan smiled. "That's good. Very good." His eyes drooped, and Frank knew he was about to drift off.

He leaned in close until he could feel his father's shallow breath on his face. He took in every wrinkle and line of his father's face, his eyelashes, the scruff on his chin and lip, and sighed.

"Goodbye, Father," he whispered. "I love you."

Ivan stirred, then drifted into a deep slumber. Frank pulled back, struggling to keep his emotions in check. Those were the last words he'd ever say to his father. At least they were *I love you*.

* * *

It felt so weird to leave his little laundry room on Wednesday morning. He'd called his boss to let him know that he wouldn't be in that day. Hinko had argued with him a full ten minutes, trying to convince him he should come to work. It was only when Frank told him his temperature was high and he needed to see a doctor, that Hinko grumbled that he expected to see him the following day.

"Yes, of course," Frank lied through a hoarse cough he'd managed to produce. "Tomorrow morning, first thing."

"Fine."

He looked back over the room and sighed. He couldn't take much with him. Whatever could fit in his pockets. He couldn't risk bringing a bag. That would look suspicious.

"We could leave on Sunday," Luka had suggested.

"No," Frank said, "That might draw attention. I'm sure most people try to cross the border on the weekend. It's more convenient."

Luka and Petar had agreed, so they decided to leave midweek. However, Frank couldn't go without seeing his *Majka* one last time. It would be difficult not to cry, but he had to do his best to not let on or his mother would certainly talk him out of it. Josip would probably understand, but would Mila? His little sister was just twelve. So sweet and innocent. What would she think when she realized that one of her brothers left the country, never to return?

This is going to be difficult.

He boarded the train and looked out the window, saying goodbye to the city that had been his home for the last five years. If Frank were being honest with himself, he never liked living in the city; but as he realized he might never see it again, he felt a sudden sensation of loss. It hadn't all been bad.

He walked from the train station to the farm, rolling up his sleeves as the morning sun beat down on him. By the time he reached his childhood home, he'd worked up a sweat. He was immediately and happily greeted by Mila and *Majka*. Josip and the uncles were out in the field but would be back for lunch before long.

The next two hours flew by too fast for Frank's liking. He was acutely aware of each word spoken by each member of his family. He couldn't shake the feeling that this would be the last contact, the last words he'd hear from them for

CHAPTER NINE

some time, maybe forever. If he was successful and actually made it across the border, it would be years before he could safely return. And if he didn't make it, he might spend the rest of his life in prison. Or he'd be shot dead.

He felt self-doubt well up deep within him yet again. Was he making the right decision? Was it truly worth the risk? As he watched Mila and *Majka* chat amiably over lunch about hair ribbons and which spice would be best to use for that evening's stew, he felt a lump in his throat. Yet he knew he had to leave. He had to try to make it in a sector of the world where he might have a chance for true prosperity.

After his uncles and brother left to return to the field, he stood up.

"I'm afraid I need to leave, too," he said reluctantly.

"But why?" Mila asked, looking deep into his eyes.

Frank smiled at her and ruffled her hair. She came up to his shoulders, sprouting skyward with each passing year. "I need to visit Luka today."

"How is it that you had the day off?" *Majka* asked, a puzzled look crossing her face. "I can't see that boss of yours giving you a holiday."

Frank felt his pulse quicken. Lying to his mother was so distasteful to him, he could feel the bile rise in his throat as he spoke the untruthful words. However, his lies were as much to protect her and his family as they were to protect him.

"Hinko asked me to come to work on Sunday," he said. "I told him no, because I had plans to see you and Luka, so he offered me Wednesday in exchange. I agreed."

Majka smiled and nodded. "That makes sense."

It would sound right if it were any boss other than Hinko. But Hinko wouldn't have any qualms about insisting that he come in on a Sunday without offering another day off in exchange. Fortunately his family didn't know how awful Hinko was, and they bought his story.

Frank knew he needed to leave immediately if he wanted to catch the correct train to Maribor, but his feet felt rooted to the floor of his family's kitchen. He tried to absorb all the scents, sounds and sights at once to commit them to memory.

"I need to go," he finally said. The last word caught in his throat like a nasty piece of meat. "I wish I could stay a little longer."

"When will you come back to visit?" Mila asked. Her young voice was bright with love for her brother and her eyes shone as she gazed into his.

"I don't know," he said honestly.

A few years. Again, he felt that lump in his throat.

"There's a concert in two weeks," *Majka* said. "Maybe you can come back then?"

He looked at his little sister. "Maybe." *Another lie.*

"Please?" Mila said.

"We'll see," Frank said as he made his way to the front door. He had to leave before he began to question his decision. As he jogged down the road, he realized he needed to quicken his pace if he were going to make it to the train station on time.

He turned back and saw that Mila and *Majka* had come out to watch him. He gave them a shaky smile before he started running for the station in earnest.

Chapter Ten

As the train pulled into the Maribor station, Frank's whole body stiffened. The screech of the train's brakes was nearly drowned out by the rush of blood in his ears. Scanning the platform, he saw Luka standing there. Alone.

Where is Petar?

Frank started to stand up, checked himself, and sat back down. If anyone noticed the strange maneuver, they didn't say anything. The people on the train were quiet, lost in their own thoughts.

The train stopped and more than half of the passengers got off. It was then that Petar came out from the shadows to fall in behind Luka. Frank let out his pent-up breath and smiled. Good, they were both here.

They boarded a few cars ahead, so he couldn't see his friends as the train started moving, which increased his nerves. However, it wasn't long before they entered his train car and greeted him with a smile. Then Luka sat beside him while Petar took an empty seat across the aisle.

Looking around the car, Frank scanned the new arrivals and wondered where they were all going. Not many people went north from Maribor. The border was only twenty kilometers or so away.

A thin, frail man was the only passenger to enter the cabin when the train stopped at Košaki.

Frank wiped his hands on his pants legs and tried to keep his legs from bouncing up and down. One down, two to go.

His heart was hammering in his chest, and he was relieved that Luka and Petar chose to remain silent.

A few minutes later, the man who'd just boarded craned his neck around to look at the three of them. Chills of fear shot through Frank as he willed the man to leave them alone. However, that wasn't to be. The man stood up and stretched, then walked over to them.

"Luka Herceg? Is that you?" the man said with a wide smile that revealed rotted teeth.

Luka gulped and nodded in a way that looked pained. Petar stared at his lap, while Frank studied the man. He seemed harmless enough as long as Luka didn't lose his cool.

The diminutive man leaned against the empty seat of the row ahead of them. "Josip. Josip Vidović," he said with a small chuckle. "I'm not surprised that you don't remember me. You were a tiny tot last time I visited your parents. How are they?"

Luka pulled a handkerchief from his pocket, wiped his brow, and said, "They're fine, just fine." His voice sounded higher pitched than it normally did. Frank groaned inwardly.

Keep it together Luka.

"Well, that's good to hear," Josip said. "So, where are you three going this fine day?"

Luka made a sound that sounded more like a croak than anything else. Frank's mind whirred and spun in a dizzying way. Why hadn't they discussed what to say if anyone asked where they were going? That would have been helpful right about now.

Frank cleared his throat and said quietly, "We have some friends in Cirknica."

"That's the last stop before…" Josip's voice trailed off and he tilted his head to the left.

The train lurched to the side as the conductor came into the car. Josip quickly found his seat, looked back at the trio, then turned away to look out the window.

CHAPTER TEN

Frank held his breath as he wondered if the man might give them away. He watched as Josip handed the conductor a ticket. The conductor punched it and handed it back. The two said a few words to each other, but Frank couldn't hear from his position. When the conductor turned back, he continued down the car just giving a glance to the three.

Frank's whole body felt much lighter when the conductor exited the car in search of other newly boarded passengers.

Five minutes later Josip stood up and exited the train at Pesnica train station. Before doing so he gave Luka a small smile and nod, which was returned with a smile. Frank gave him a grateful wave and hoped he was reading the man correctly.

One more stop. Just one more stop.

They planned to exit at Cirknica, the last stop before the border and travel the rest of the way on foot. Luka's map showed a clear path from Cirknica to the border, about three and a half kilometers long. He was confident they would be able to make it.

The train sat at the station while the three men remained in their seats.

Luka looked around. "There are others here on the train. We'll be fine."

Frank felt beads of sweat form as he glanced around. Luka was right. There was a handful of other passengers. Frank wondered why the others were going to Cirknica, and if anyone would be questioned.

As the minutes ticked by and the train continued to sit at the station, Frank considered getting off. He recalled Petar's map. Though it was a lot further to walk to the border from here than from Cirknica, close to ten kilometers, it might arouse less suspicion.

As they continued to sit in their seats and wait, Frank wiped his hands against his pants again. Just then his eye caught a movement outside the window, and his breath caught in the back of his throat. Four armed and uniformed officers walked purposefully toward the train.

Frank couldn't stop his whole body from trembling. There was no doubt in his mind that the officers were coming for them. They should have gotten off the train with the other passengers.

Had Josip turned them in? No, he wouldn't have given them that look if he had. That parting look had said volumes. If Frank had been a mind reader, he would have said Josip had been wishing them good luck.

Frank's mind turned to mush as two of the officers stepped onto their train car. Their uniforms were clean, pressed, and both were clean shaven. They appeared to be in their early twenties, just like him and his friends. Maybe they'd have some understanding.

One by one, the officers asked each passenger for identification, then asked them a series of questions about their destination. When they stepped up to Frank and his friends, the officer with a long scar running down his left cheek said curtly, "Identification?"

They produced their cards and waited. Frank studied the scar and wondered how he'd received it. Looked like a knife wound. He shuddered.

The officer turned to Luka and Petar. "You live in Maribor?"

"T-that's right," Luka stammered.

The officer frowned at them. "Stand up. All of you."

The three stood up in unison. Frank glanced at Petar and Luka and groaned internally. They trembled, looked down, and were growing more and more pale by the second.

In contrast, Frank smiled at the officer and looked him in the eye. "Good day, sir," he said cheerfully, thankful that his voice didn't catch.

CHAPTER TEN

The officer cocked his head. "And you're from Zagreb."

"That's right."

"What brings you three all the way up to Cirknica?"

"U-uh," Petar said, while Luka just stared at his shoes.

"I can explain," Frank said.

The man squinted at Frank. "Come with me, then," he said.

Frank looked at his friends. "All of us?"

"No, just you," he said, and motioned for Frank to follow him.

Frank didn't want to be separated from his friends, but he couldn't think of a reason to object. Besides, objecting was useless and would only increase suspicions.

As Frank followed the officer, he looked at the other passengers still seated on the train. The men and women carefully avoided any eye contact, as if they anticipated his removal from the train. They probably lived in Cirknica and didn't want to get tangled up with Frank and his friends, who were obviously in trouble.

When the officer reached the front of the car, he leaned against the compartment door. "Where are you three going?"

Frank again cursed himself that he hadn't insisted that his friends come up with a logical reason why they would be traveling from Maribor to the last station before the border to Austria.

Frank forced his shoulders to relax and gave the officer a wide grin. "I don't know about the other two. I was on my way to Cirknica when they got on at Maribor. I was happy to run into them. We're all friends, you know."

The officer looked back at the others being interrogated by his fellow officer. "How do you know them?" he asked.

Frank shrugged. "I worked with Luka at Lovric Shoes in Zagreb." Might as well go with the truth as much as possible. "The other guy is his cousin. Petar."

The officer nodded and looked back at Frank. "Continue. So, why are *you* going toward the border?"

Frank felt a thrill of fear shoot up his spine. *Calm down.* "I didn't think about that. See, I met this girl. She asked me to meet her in Cirknica."

A glint of understanding crept into the man's eye. "A girl, huh?"

"Yeah," Frank said, pulling out a small card with a name and address on it. "See, she gave me this and asked me to come today."

With trembling hands he handed it to the officer. He'd made this card when he'd woken up in the middle of the night with the idea. He'd written it out, then tucked it into his pants pocket. Just in case. At the time he'd laughed at his overactive imagination, but now he was thankful he'd thought of it. Looking back at Luka and Petar, he knew they hadn't come up with any plausible story. They were both being escorted off the train.

Frank caught Luka's eye as he stepped off. The look of terror made his blood run cold. What would happen to them? He closed his eyes and hoped they'd just be returned to Maribor. He hoped the officer might take pity on two youths his own age and just send them home.

It was unlikely.

"It's a workday," the man said, tilting his head. "How did you get the day off?"

Frank bowed his head, trying his best to look contrite. "When a beautiful girl asks you to meet her, it's hard to say no. I told my boss I was sick." He then looked up at the officer and gave him what he hoped would pass for a smitten look.

The man gave him a leering grin. He glanced at the card. "Ana. Pretty name."

"Yeah," Frank said, wiping his hands on his pant legs.

"What does she look like?"

CHAPTER TEN

Frank closed his eyes and thought of Ljubica. He felt himself flush at the thought of the only girl who had ever really caught his eye. She was gorgeous. As he remembered that one day he'd spent with her, he said, "She has long dark hair the color of night. And large, expressive eyes. She is just the most beautiful woman I've ever seen. I plan to marry her one day."

Although he was fabricating the story about the girl at the last stop for the officer, he drew on his love of Ljubica to lend authenticity to the tale. After all, this whole thing would only work if the man believed him; this story had to ring true.

Ljubica. Just thinking of her warm smile made his heart flutter. He allowed himself to get caught up in his feelings for her, swaying a bit on his feet as his heart swelled with emotion.

He needed to reach Austria first, then he'd find a way to help her cross the border. He'd offer her his hand in marriage and do everything he could to convince her. He had no idea how she felt about him, but first he needed to be worthy of her love.

"She sounds delightful," the man said.

Frank opened his eyes and grinned. "So, you'll let me go?" Hope surged within Frank's breast. Was it possible that this would work?

"Sure," the man said. "I'm nothing if not a romantic."

Frank felt as he had when he'd won foot races as a boy. He thanked the Lord, who had obviously been smiling on him that day. He was going to make it across the border, after all.

"But I need to go with you," the officer said.

As if the sky had opened up and dumped a bucket of cold water on his head, Frank's hopes and dreams were dashed in that instant. He nodded and gulped back his fear. How was that going to work? What would the officer do when they reached the stop, and no pretty girl was waiting for him?

"Of course," Frank said. Then he added for good measure, "Just don't steal her from me. Girls love a man in uniform."

The man laughed. "I have my own girl," he said. "Come, join me in the station. I'm due to catch a later train. You'll have to stay with me. We can play a game of pool while we wait."

Pool?

Frank felt lightheaded as he numbly followed the man into the station and into a side room, where there was an old, beat-up pool table. The felt was well worn, and there was only one cue for them to share.

The officer broke while Frank looked around the room. He froze when he spotted a large map on the wall. It wasn't as detailed as the one that Luka had, but it showed him where he needed to go.

"Your turn," the officer said.

Frank smiled and looked at the balls. He hadn't been paying attention, but now he noticed the man had knocked in the yellow solid. So he was stripes. He reminded himself that winning wasn't the objective. Although he knew his way around a pool table, Frank needed to be sure he didn't win.

He aimed at the number 10 ball and narrowly missed the corner pocket. It was hard to miss on purpose.

"Tough break," the officer said with a gleam in his eye. While his attention was fixed on the table, Frank stole another look at the map, doing his best to commit it to memory. Cirknica was only a few kilometers from the border. He had to remember to veer slightly west. If he walked straight north or even went off a little east, it would add a good kilometer or two to his journey. And he'd have to cross a river. No, it was far better to head a little west.

Frank didn't risk studying the map any further but focused on giving the officer a decent game while losing. When they were done, the officer slapped him on the back. "Good game."

"Thank you," Frank said. "The better man won."

CHAPTER TEN

The man chuckled at that. "Rack them up. Let's play again."

The sun hung low in the western sky by the time the officer was ready to leave. "Better get back on the train and meet that girl of yours. I can't wait to see her."

Frank nodded and brushed the sweat from his hands against his shirt. His mind raced, trying to figure out what to do next. What was he going to do when he got to the train station and there was no girl? He could tell the officer that they'd arrived so late that the girl had probably left. But then the man might decide to go to the mythical address on the card and that wouldn't do. Frank took a deep breath. He didn't have long to come up with a plan.

Chapter Eleven

As the train continued to speed along, Frank's heart pounded in his chest. The officer was so close to him, he could smell the man's body odor. He figured they were minutes away from Cirknica station and he still didn't have a way to get rid of his guard. He'd hoped the officer would give him a little space, maybe leave the train car for a moment, but no such luck. Frank sighed and looked out the window at the shadowy landscape. He had to come up with a plan.

"You look eager," the man said. "What was your love's name again?"

"Ljubica," Frank said without thinking. Then he froze in shock, his eyes widening as he realized his error. He'd completely forgotten the name he'd given to the fictitious woman on the card.

Maybe the officer wouldn't notice.

The man wrinkled his brow and took the little card Frank had given him out of his pocket. "Wait. This girl's name's Ana," he said.

"Sorry, I meant Ana."

The officer's eyes turned hard. "There is no Ana. Is there?"

Without thinking, Frank bolted away from the officer. He had to get to the compartment door. Moments later he felt himself catapulted forward. Frank grabbed at a seatback to his right, but it slipped from his hand, and he crashed to the floor. He turned to get up and was instantly thrown back

CHAPTER ELEVEN

to the ground by a fist to his face. Shards of pain burst from his lip as a flash of light momentarily blinded him.

He didn't have time to register the taste of blood but flailed his foot out to kick the officer. He could hear his grunt of pain and thanked the Lord that he'd done a little damage.

He kicked again and scooted back to give himself enough room to get up. The officer grabbed Frank's left foot, making getting up impossible. Propping himself up with his arms, he shot out his right foot to make contact. The man grunted but didn't release his shoe.

Frank pulled back his right foot and kicked again and again to no avail. The man pulled Frank's leg and grabbed his calf with a grip that felt like a claw.

I can't give up!

Frank continued to pummel the man with kicks to his head and torso, hoping and praying one would weaken the man's vice grip. Finally, when the man looked up toward Frank, he managed to land a kick squarely on his nose. It was a solid kick.

The man immediately loosened his hold and cried out in pain. Frank wriggled out of his hold, scooted back as fast as he could, and managed to get to his feet. He looked back at the officer and saw what looked like pints of blood gushing from his nose.

He paused for a moment, looking at the officer. He'd never hurt another person before and immediately felt guilty. He curbed his impulse to go to the man and help him. If he did, he'd wind up in prison or perhaps dead. No, he needed to jump off the train.

Jump off the train.

What was the chance that he'd make it?

Frank considered the practicality of jumping and suddenly realized the injuries he could sustain from the impact with the ground. His whole body reacted with a tense series of prickly pain as if all his nerve endings were protesting at the same moment.

When the officer stood up, pulling a rag from his pocket to apply to the wound, Frank turned to the connecting door. Behind him he heard the officer call for backup on his portable radio.

Frank pushed on the door and felt the breeze of the early evening hit his face just as the sun sunk beneath the horizon. He had another few minutes or so before darkness set in. Just then the train lurched, and he heard the squeal of the brakes. The train pulled sharply and was slowing down.

This is my chance.

He glanced back and saw that the officer had his hand on the handle on the other side of the compartment door. His scarred face was deep red, and his eyes told Frank that if he caught him, Frank probably wouldn't make it to prison. He'd be dead within minutes.

The compartment door opened, just as the train was coming out of a wide turn, still slowing. Frank jumped, barely escaping the officer's grasp.

Behind him, Frank heard the officer curse. "*Jebote!*"

Feeling the exhilaration that comes from soaring through the air, he tried not to think about what the impact with the earth would feel like. As he plummeted down, he realized that fortune was smiling on him. The ground looked to be a sort of grassy hill rather than a rocky cliff. He quickly curled into a ball and rolled down into the gully, where he lay still, looking up at the train cars. He wondered if the guards would jump as he did or if they would wait until the train stopped at the station. But that would take a few minutes.

No time to wonder!

He stood up and took off running as fast as he could. As the evening turned darker and darker, Frank was thankful that the moon was nearly full, and the sky was clear. Another

CHAPTER ELEVEN

stroke of luck. Maybe. He would be able to see, but then again, the people chasing him could spot him easier as well.

Looking around, he made out a group of trees to his right. That would hide him better than the open field he found himself in. He glanced back to see if anyone was following. The wind picked up and hit him full in the face. No one was there yet. He turned to face forward and felt the wind pushing him from behind, as if rooting for him. If only he could fly!

Frank refocused his attention on the grouping of trees and ran full force. In his eagerness, he missed the stump jutting out of the ground just in front of him and found himself sailing through the air. He landed awkwardly on his right foot and fell to the ground. When he tried to stand, he winced in pain. He took another step and nearly cried out.

Was it broken or sprained?

Only time would tell.

Frank continued to hobble forward as fast as he could. Damn, but the ankle was slowing him down. He wondered how far he could get if it was broken. He suppressed the urge to cry out in pain.

By the time he made it to the edge of the woods, he heard the bark of one dog, then another and another. How many were there? It sounded like four or five, but it was hard to tell. He briefly wondered if this was how a fox felt when the hounds were after him in an old-fashioned British hunt.

Frank took a few faltering steps into the forest, then paused behind the cover of the trees and squinted across the field. He could see the shadowy figures of a dozen or so men running toward him. He froze in shock. He had no idea so many officers had been aboard that train. He groaned, turned, and began to slowly stumble through the small forest. It was much darker beneath the cover of the trees. Although that made traversing the woods difficult, the blackness might also help to conceal him. He needed a place to hide and something that would hopefully also mask his scent.

How many guns were there?

He shook his head. He couldn't think about how badly the odds were stacked against him. He grimaced. He could feel the sweat dripping from him. That would be a problem. He needed his clothes, but they probably reeked. He realized he needed to be downwind of the dogs, so he continued to move with the wind at his back. As long as it was blowing behind him, he'd have a much better chance of escaping the dogs.

Frank considered climbing a tree but figured that was too risky. If it didn't work and somehow the dogs zeroed in on his scent, he'd be quickly caught, with no way out. There would be no escape once they got him down from the tree.

He heard the men and dogs getting closer and closer. The crunch of the leaves under his feet sounded like cymbals crashing. It was impossible to be stealthy in this forest, so he slowed down. He found a spot where the trees were denser and lay down on the forest floor. He covered himself with branches and leaves and hoped the wind would continue to blow in the right direction.

Buried, he could feel something crawling up his leg, but he didn't dare move. The wind continued to pick up, making a rustling sound that permeated the forest. He steadied his breathing and waited.

Frank could hear the shouts of the men and the ear-piercing barking all around him. One man was maybe three meters from his feet calling to the others. For a moment Frank was certain that the man had found his location. He almost jumped up from his hiding spot but realized there would be no way out if he did. He wasn't much of a gambler, but he knew that his chances were much better if he remained still.

Another man joined the first, and Frank strained to hear their conversation.

CHAPTER ELEVEN

"The wind is too strong. The dogs can't catch his scent." He didn't recognize the voice.

"*Jebote*," the other cursed, his voice slightly muffled. That was a voice he'd not soon forget. It would probably plague his nightmares for decades to come. It was the officer with the now-bloody and possibly broken nose. "If only I had a piece of his clothes. I had the *šupak* in my hands and I just let him go."

"Too bad."

"Yeah, too bad."

Frank then heard the sound of the two men slogging through the leaves, loudly cursing as they trudged through the forest, retreating. He strained his ears, but he could no longer make out their words as they moved farther away. Finally, after what seemed like a long time, he could only hear the faint sound of their voices and the barking of the dogs.

Frank continued to wait, hidden beneath the pile of leaves, for a long while after it got quiet. He didn't dare move. He could imagine the man with the nasty scar hiding in the shadows, hoping to fool Frank and draw him out. He did his best to make out the officers' voices but couldn't discern anything beyond the wind.

It was only after it was completely silent for many minutes that Frank tentatively sat up. He made his way back to the edge of the forest. Still hidden behind the trees, he watched as the train began to move again. It was a miracle that he hadn't been caught. Frank leaned back against the tree and sighed in relief.

Chapter Twelve

Frank looked back at the tracks. Up the line, in the far distance, he could see some lights and figured that was Cirknica. He figured that was north and noted that he had jumped off on the western side of the train. So if he continued to follow the tracks north while veering a bit to the west, he should come to the Austrian border. He estimated that it was about four kilometers away since he had jumped off the train before it reached Cirknica. Slowly he began to walk, mindful to stay in the shadows of the forest.

Frank continued to walk for another thirty minutes; it was the longest thirty minutes of his life. His ankle was killing him. He wished he could stop and rest for a moment but knew that wasn't wise. No matter how severe the pain, it was a fraction of what he'd experience if he were captured and put in Goli Otok. With each step, he winced in pain and wondered whether his ankle was, in fact, broken. It had swollen to the size of a large sugar beet.

He emerged from the small forest and crossed over farmland. He wondered what time it was, not sure how long he'd been hiding on the forest floor, quaking in the darkness. Although it had felt like an hour, he was certain his perception was off. In reality, it had probably been only fifteen or twenty minutes.

He saw a large barn silhouetted in the moonlight and sighed. He hadn't made much progress. If he stopped here, maybe he could regroup when the sun came up and make

CHAPTER TWELVE

sure he was on the correct path. On the other hand, stopping now would give the police time to find him, if they were looking for him. He would lose the cover of night and be in the open for anyone to see.

Frank took five steps forward and realized there was no way he'd be able to travel the rest of the way to the border. He hobbled to the barn and was grateful to find that the huge door was open just enough so that he could squeeze inside. He didn't think he had the strength to push it open. He waited a moment for his eyes to adjust to the dark interior.

To the right were three stalls. Two housed one horse each; the third was empty. He made his way slowly to the third and looked inside. He immediately took a step back as he pinched his nose; it was filled with dung. He turned around and found a clean corner to lay down in.

Frank had just settled under a horse blanket and closed his eyes when he heard the large barn door slide open. He opened his eyes and saw a man with a lantern. Moonlight and lamplight spilled into the barn and Frank knew there would be no hiding from the owner.

Frank could see the weathered face of a man whose body position looked stiff. Frank couldn't discern any features from that distance but could see the man had short dark hair and a scruffy beard. Frank held his breath for a moment, his heart pounding in his chest. He struggled to sit up.

"Hello," he called out tentatively.

As the man moved forward with the use of a cane, Frank could see that he was probably in his sixties or seventies.

"Who's there?" the man said. Frank could hear the fear in the man's voice.

"I'm Frank," he said, smiling in a way that he hoped might put the man at ease. "I hope you don't mind if I stay the night. I won't be any trouble."

The man grunted and continued forward. "I do mind," he said.

Frank sighed and stood up, crying out in the pain as he put weight on his bad ankle. "I'm sorry. I was injured."

The man shuffled forward and stopped near Frank. "I'm sorry to hear that."

Frank smiled again. "Thank you."

"Why are you here?" The man gave him a look that clearly said he didn't trust Frank.

Frank's mind raced with possible explanations he could give the old man. As the seconds ticked by, Frank knew that any answer other than the truth would not be believed simply because of the delay in answering. After all, truth flowed from the tongue easily, whereas lies needed time to be created. If Frank opted for anything other than the truth, it would sound false and would breed distrust. Frank couldn't risk that. The man lived a few kilometers from the border. Frank probably wasn't the first who'd crossed his land on foot in search of freedom.

This man, at this moment, was the most important man in the world to Frank. This farmer held his future in his gnarled hands. "I'm heading for the border," Frank finally said.

His words hung like spider webs in the dusty old barn. The man regarded him with his brown eyes as each held the other's gaze. Finally he gave Frank a nod. "You came from the train station."

It was more of a statement than a question, but Frank nodded nonetheless. It was easier to agree than to go into the whole story. "Yes, sir." He hated how tentative and unsure his voice sounded. He'd have preferred it if he came across confident.

"That's the way most young men come," the old man said with a small smile.

CHAPTER TWELVE

Frank relaxed his shoulders and allowed himself to fall back onto a hay bale. "There've been others?"

"More than I can count."

"So, can I stay the night?"

"Yes. You hungry?"

Frank grinned up at the man. "Starving!"

The man nodded. "Wait here. I'll get you something. I have some leftover stew from dinner. I'll heat it up for you."

"That would be wonderful."

Frank watched the man make his way slowly through the barn door to the small house about twenty meters away. Seated on the hay bale, he waited, the minutes passing slowly. Frank began to worry. What if the man had just said what he said to keep him there? He stood and limped to the barn entrance. Was it possible that this man was in fact riding out to alert the authorities?

No, the two horses were still there. But what about the third stable with the fresh manure? Where was the third horse? No, he would have heard the galloping sound.

Unless the man had walked the third horse down the dirt road a ways.

Panic welled up within Frank's chest as he considered his options. Could he trust this man he didn't know not to go to the authorities? He had to decide whether to simply wait to see if this man would actually bring him dinner or make a run for it. After all, he still had time to leave. It would take the old man time to find the authorities and time for them to arrive.

Frank was so torn that he could feel his body lurch forward, then back as if it were having its own debate. He looked down at his swollen ankle and shook his head. It made the decision for him. He winced his way back to the hay bale and sat to await his fate. He dropped his head into his hands.

The other deciding factor was that he still didn't know for sure which way was north. He didn't know which way to go.

"You OK?" a raspy voice came from the doorway.

Frank's head jerked up as he looked into the old farmer's face. "Yeah," he said. He looked at the man's hands to find a bowl with steam rising from it. He felt a tremendous sensation of airy lightness as he stood up. "Thank you. That looks delicious."

The man cackled. "I don't think anyone's ever described my cooking that way," he said as he made his way over to Frank, "but it's not burnt. That's something."

Frank accepted the bowl and the spoon, along with a piece of bread that looked freshly baked. He sat down and nearly burned his mouth on the first bite. He didn't care. The hot liquid felt so good going down. "It *is* delicious. Thank you!"

The man smiled. "It's just me here. I cook with what I have. Chicken and vegetables. And a few herbs I manage to grow when they're not eaten by the rabbits."

Frank nodded as he hungrily ate spoon after spoon of the broth. He bit into the dark brown bread and sighed with pleasure. It was just like the bread his *Majka* made.

Being able to relax in front of this man, telling him the truth was a relief. And having a belly full of warm stew, he felt blessed. Frank looked up at the man. "I'm embarrassed to ask this, but can you tell me which way is north?"

The man cocked his head to the right and turned to point directly out of the barn. "Why, that's north. Just keep going that way, and you'll find the border."

Frank's shoulders sagged. The man was pointing in the direction that Frank had just come from. He'd gone the wrong way. He groaned and leaned his head back against the barn wall. That meant he was probably five to seven kilometers away from the border.

CHAPTER TWELVE

"So, how far from the border am I?" he whispered, not really wanting to know.

"Not far," the man said. "Just a little over two kilometers. If you follow that path."

Frank sat up with a jerk. Two kilometers? Cirknica was about twice that distance and he'd jumped off near that station. So that meant he *had* been heading north. His head swam as he tried to wrap his wits around the conflicting information.

He stood and pointed out the door. Confusion made his head reel. "You're saying that's north?"

"Yes. That's the direction you should go," the man said.

"Thank you," Frank said with a nod. "Then that's what I'll do."

The man turned to leave. He called back over his shoulder. "Stay as long as you like. Get a good night's sleep."

Frank nodded and watched him go out the barn door. He went back to the corner and lay back down. The old man must be confused. It was late and he'd just pointed in the wrong direction. At least Frank knew now which way to go.

Frank willed himself to relax and allow sleep to overtake him. He needed the rest. Hopefully, his foot would heal by morning.

Chapter Thirteen

Frank awoke with a start and sat up. His heart was beating so loudly, he was sure the old man could hear it in his house. He leaned back on his arms. It was still dark, and Frank had no idea what time it was. How long had he slept?

He'd woken from a particularly vicious dream where German shepherds were chasing him, biting relentlessly at his right ankle. As if on cue, his ankle throbbed. He pulled up his right pant leg and groaned. He touched the swelling tenderly and winced. Curling into a ball, his head against his knee, he felt like whimpering. Then he heard a sound that made him tense.

Had that been a dog's bark?

No, it couldn't be. That was just a remnant from his dream. Then he heard it again. And again. A chorus of barks that sounded like it was far away but coming closer.

Frank scrambled to his feet. The adrenaline that coursed through him wiped out the pain in his ankle. He raced to the door and heard the sound again. The barks were ripping through the silence of the night air.

Frank groaned as he considered his options. It became clear to him that the old man had waited and called the authorities as soon as he thought Frank was asleep. That explained the lie. Of course the man had known which way was north. No farmer would make that mistake. He knew which direction the sun came up each morning.

CHAPTER THIRTEEN

Frank cursed himself for being a trusting fool. Now he'd pay the price.

He looked at the house and wondered if the man would come out. He couldn't see any shadows in the windows. The old man was probably hiding in some closet, being the coward that he was. Frank took off running, ignoring the pain. He couldn't afford the luxury of taking his time. He looked back to see if anyone was following him. No. Not yet.

Frank headed for a small copse of trees just north of the farm. It would offer better cover than the open field in the bright moonlight. Exhausted, he continued onward and wondered how soon the men with the dogs would catch up to him.

Frank stopped and turned back to look at the barn. Maybe, just maybe, he'd get lucky. If the old man believed that he'd fooled Frank, he'd send the police in the wrong direction. He'd tell them that Frank went south. Frank smiled. That would be a stroke of luck. Ironic that the man's attempt at deception might just be Frank's saving grace.

He felt a surge of hope and strength. He ran across two more fields and into another forest. He strained to hear if anyone was chasing him. He couldn't hear any dogs. That was something.

How much further was it to the border?

Then Frank had a chilling thought. Would there be guards at the border?

If he understood the map that he'd seen at the train station correctly, the official border was in a forest. But which one? He couldn't be sure. It was best to just continue onward. As he stumbled over a large root, and then another, he realized he probably needed to slow down.

This was a large forest. Frank hoped he had his bearings and that he was still heading north. He continued moving until the forest opened onto another farm. The sky was beginning to brighten as he stepped out of the shadows of the trees and onto the grass.

Where am I?

He looked around and saw a man and woman doing familiar chores. The woman was milking a cow, while the man was feeding slop to the pigs. Most likely they'd been up for an hour already.

Frank stood and watched them for a while, wondering if he should approach them. Although the last encounter with the old farmer hadn't gone well, he was certain that most people wouldn't wish him harm. He had to trust others. He couldn't give up now.

The adrenaline had lessened, and the pain in his foot was coming back full force. He hobbled over to the couple, who stopped what they were doing to look up at him. The woman rose from her milking stool to stand by her husband.

"*Guten Morgen,*" the man called out.

Frank stopped, his mind reeling. *German*. He was speaking German! Although Frank didn't know many words in this language, he did recognize this familiar greeting.

"*Guten Morgen,*" he replied. Then he sighed and said, "Do you speak Serbo-Croatian?"

Frank held his breath while he waited for their answer. Had he crossed the border? If not, he had at least to be close.

"Yes," the woman said. "Have you come from Yugoslavia, then?"

Frank nodded. "I've been trying to get across the border all night."

The man smiled. "Well, I'm happy to tell you that you've made it. You're in Austria. We get a few people visiting us from your country now and then."

Frank felt a joy infuse him unlike anything he'd ever experienced before. He'd made it! He never had to worry

CHAPTER THIRTEEN

about Tito's hounds or police ever again. This was the first day of a new life. He was ready!

"Thank you," he murmured. "Thank you!"

Waves and waves of realizations hit him so hard his knees gave way and he collapsed to the ground. Tears of joy streamed down his face. He could say whatever he wanted to say now. He had freedom of speech. He had the freedom to earn what he could potentially earn, a true ability to buy what he wanted. This was it. He'd made it. He could be as successful as his talent allowed.

The man and woman looked at each other and smiled. They gave him a moment, then the woman said softly, "You're probably hungry. And thirsty. I'll make you some breakfast."

The man leaned down to help Frank back up to his feet. Frank winced as he leaned on his right foot.

The woman clucked. "And I'll look at that ankle. I have some bandages in the house."

Frank leaned on the man and said, "I'd be very grateful."

"After breakfast, we'll take you into town," the woman said. "You can talk to the police."

Frank pulled away so sharply that he nearly fell over. The man looked reproachfully at his wife before looking back at Frank. "Now, now, don't worry. The Austrian police will help you. I promise."

Frank relaxed. "Of course."

"It will take some time, but you'll see things are different here," he said.

Frank nodded. "Thank you."

* * *

As he sat in the small but clean police station, Frank could immediately tell the difference. The officer in front of him was polite and fortunately spoke his language. After the preliminary questions were out of the way, the man asked, "Why did you leave Yugoslavia?"

Frank paused and remembered what the farmer and his wife had said. They'd coached him on this point, for which he was now very grateful. He knew this was a very important question. Answer it wrong and he'd be on the next train back.

The man had said, "If you say that you can't get a decent job in Yugoslavia, they'll send you back. They don't want that."

"So, what do I say?" Frank had asked. He'd felt panic well up inside him. What if he made a mistake and, after all that he'd been through, he was just shipped home?

"Just say that you don't like the government," the man had told him. "That will be enough."

Frank took a deep breath and looked the officer in the eye. "President Tito doesn't allow anyone freedom to think their own thoughts or say what they feel. If you criticize him, you're put in jail. I was recently questioned by police there because I said I felt Goli Otok was inhumane. I nearly lost my life for that one comment."

Frank held his breath and waited. The man nodded. "So you don't like Communism?"

"That's right," Frank said.

The officer continued to ask him questions about his work and life back in Yugoslavia. He seemed impressed by Frank's accomplishment and experience as a cobbler.

After an hour, the officer put all the paperwork into a file. He looked up at Frank and gave him a wide smile. "Welcome to Austria, Mr. Katana. Now let's find you a place to stay."

Chapter Fourteen

September 1956

It was early September and Frank was itching to move out of the barracks of the immigration camp in Graz. He'd been shipped to this city within a few days of crossing the border, along with many other refugees. He enjoyed walking through the large city with its beautiful gothic architecture.

He wasn't complaining about life in the camp. It was much better than Yugoslavia; the food was far more plentiful and there was no oppression.

After he'd settled in the camp, Frank had sent a telegram to his mother to let her know that he'd arrived safely in Austria. He hadn't been sure if it would be all right to admit such a thing openly through the telegram service. After all, others would read the message before passing it along.

He'd found a few others in the camp who had told him they had sent similar messages without incident. That gave him the confidence to let his *Majka* know. He'd follow up with more details in a letter, but it was always uncertain how long a letter would take to arrive at its destination.

Frank pulled out his DP card and sighed. He was a displaced person, but not for long. The euphoria of having succeeded in crossing the border hadn't quite dissipated, but the reality of living in a long one-room house lined with bunkbeds had put a bit of a damper on it. This lifestyle certainly lacked privacy. However, that didn't stop some of the beds from rocking and squeaking in the middle of the night.

Not only was the smell of unwashed bodies and continual flatulence by his neighbors getting to him, but he knew other people arrived daily, crossing the border to find freedom. They would also need beds and would be grateful for a chance to take his. As a result, guilt ate at him. He needed to vacate his spot.

Most refugees came from Hungary. He wished he could understand their language, as he would have loved to hear their stories. He had heard that more and more of the young people were tired of the suppression of their communist government and were considering banding together to put an end to it. Those brave men and women were staying behind. The others were crossing the border any way they could.

Frank knew his story was different. He was on a mission to not just survive but succeed in a way no one in his family had ever done. Looking around, he wondered how many others had similar goals. More than half the men in his barracks had a high school education or a specialized skill as he did. The officials had done their best to put people with some kind of training on a transport for Graz. All the others were shipped to other camps around Austria, and the overflow went to a couple of camps in Italy.

These camps were intended to be a temporary solution. Most everyone in these camps needed to leave Austria and were simply waiting for the opportunity to be shipped to another country. There, they could live out their lives and contribute with the strength of their hands and the drive in their hearts, benefiting their new country.

A sudden commotion at the door made Frank sit up. As the people in the barracks swarmed the Red Cross worker, he knew that the tall man probably had clothes. Most were

CHAPTER FOURTEEN

in the same position as Frank was—they'd arrived with what they'd worn on their backs.

By the time Frank got to the door, the clothes had all been taken. All except for one woolen gray hat. He looked around to see if anyone else might be interested in it. No one was. That probably had something to do with the small heat wave they'd been experiencing. Warm hats weren't on anyone's mind. However, he knew it would be cold soon enough and was grateful to have something to keep his head warm in the months to come.

He headed over to the kitchen to put in a few hours of dishwashing duty. All the refugees rotated through the various shifts. As he scrubbed the pots, his new friend Marko sidled up to him.

"A new wave of Hungarians showed up last night," he said.

Frank nodded. "I heard. How many?"

"Not sure. Maybe a couple dozen. They looked so thin."

The two fell silent.

All those new people meant that beds would be at a premium again.

"Have you tried to contact your mother's cousin?" Marko asked.

"No, not yet."

"Why? She might be able to put you up."

"Like I said before," Frank said with a shake of his head, "I want to be able to pay her something. I need to get some kind of job first."

"Oh, I've been meaning to tell you," Marko said. "There's a new guy who was talking about a cobbler who lost his assistant."

Frank paled. "Lost?"

"No, no, nothing like that," Marko said. "Sorry, I shouldn't have said that. Poor choice of words. No, he left for Vienna."

"Really?" Frank asked, biting his lip. It was a promising bit of news. "Which store is it?"

"I don't know."

"It's a big city with lots of shops. Might be hard to find. Maybe you can ask the guy again?"

"Sorry, I don't know where he went and didn't catch his name," Marko said.

"It's all right. I'll ask around and see what I can find."

After he finished cleaning the dishes, he headed into town. Armed with this new information, he began to ask people if they knew of a cobbler who was hiring. Most people in this town could understand him and spoke at least a smattering of Slovenian or Croatian.

At the end of the day, Frank walked into the small but thriving shop of David Gruber. He could immediately tell that this man was overworked and overwhelmed. Mr. Gruber's round face split into a wide grin when Frank explained that he was able to begin work immediately.

When he left the shop, Frank pulled out the little slip of paper from his pocket with the name and address of his mother's cousin, Ema. After asking for directions from a few people, he found the small apartment on the edge of town.

Frank raised his hand to knock and paused. What would this woman say? Well, there was only one way to find out. Feeling his heart hammer in his chest, Frank rapped on the door twice.

When a slight woman with salt and pepper hair pulled back in a long ponytail answered the door, he could immediately see the family resemblance in her eyes and nose. Smiling, he introduced himself.

He held his breath and waited for Ema to respond. He didn't have to wait long as the woman enveloped him in a warm embrace and invited him into her home. She bade him

CHAPTER FOURTEEN

to sit on her forest-green couch while she disappeared into the kitchen to make some coffee.

Looking around the room, Frank felt as if he were back on his farm in Mali Bukovec. Ema had small naïve paintings hanging on the wall in small clusters. They depicted starving peasants begging in the streets for food while a few fat Communist leaders feasted nearby. Frank admired the artist's bravery. The man had managed to find a way to express his displeasure with the system the only way he could—with oil paint and a brush. Frank's lips formed into a wry smile as he was reminded of why he had left Yugoslavia.

When Ema returned, she had a plate of *knedle* in her hands, which shook slightly. "I'd made these this morning for my grandchildren. There's enough to share."

"*Knedle.*" Frank's voice broke. Suddenly a wave of grief hit him as he thought of *Majka* and her cooking. He hoped Ema wouldn't ask him to speak any time soon. He didn't trust his voice.

Frank hadn't allowed himself to think about the people he'd left behind, keeping himself busy with tasks around the camp instead. After he'd sent the initial telegram home, he'd followed it with a letter telling his mother and siblings the details about his decision to leave. He'd hoped they'd understand but knew deep down his mother would be worried sick about her baby.

Ema kept her head bent and Frank knew she'd probably caught his emotional reaction and was giving him time. He was grateful.

She handed him a plate with two potato dumplings and smiled, "It's your mother's recipe."

He grinned. "Plum?"

"Of course."

He took a bite and sighed with pleasure. "Thank you!"

She pulled a *knedle* onto another small plate. "Where are you staying?"

"I'm in an immigration camp a few kilometers away."

She wrinkled her nose. "How do you like it there?"

He looked at her and shrugged. "It's fine."

She gave him a lopsided smile. "Is it?"

He paused, then returned her smile. "It's better than the alternative."

Ema looked around her apartment. "I just have one bedroom and this room, but you're welcome to stay if you want."

Frank felt his shoulders relax. "That would be great. I just found employment so I can chip in until I can book passage to Australia."

"Australia?" Ema asked giving a shudder of disgust. "Why would you want to go there?"

He felt the sting of fear shoot up his spine at her words. "What? What's wrong with Australia?"

"Nothing, if you like large bugs and snakes. Lots of snakes."

Frank shook his head slowly. "I hate snakes."

"Me, too. And they aren't like they are here. Slimy but harmless. No, in Australia, they'll kill you."

"How do you know all of this?"

"A few friends emigrated last year and wrote me all about it. Even drew a few pictures in the letter. They said the snakes' venom is worse than anywhere in the world. Those slithery things have a bad temper and seem to go after people. And you got to watch your step and look in your shoes whenever you take them off because half the time insects will make their home inside."

Frank felt his heart race and knew he had to find another solution. First thing tomorrow, he'd go to the camp officials and change his request to America or Canada.

CHAPTER FOURTEEN

"And my friends said the summers, which are at the time of our winter, are hotter than any desert you can imagine. A few days were almost fifty degrees," she went on. "Can you imagine going out in that?"

"No," Frank said. "I'm so glad you told me. You just saved my life in more ways than one!"

"Well, good," Ema said with a nod. "You move in here as soon as you're ready. All I can offer you is the couch."

"That would be perfect," Frank said.

Chapter Fifteen

Frank fell into a comfortable good routine of working for Mr. Gruber six days a week, then coming back to Ema's delicious homecooked Croatian meals. He tried to give her money, but she wouldn't take it.

"You've got to save for Canada," was all she'd say.

Canada.

He wasn't sure how he felt about the cold country, but he knew Australia was out of the question. Besides the venomous snakes, the place was apparently crawling with all sorts of nasty bugs, some of which stung or bit you. How could he have thought this would be a paradise? No, Canada was definitely a better choice.

Frank didn't like continually taking food from Ema. She had a kind heart and would just as soon go hungry than not feed his empty belly. In an effort to chip in, he bought bags of groceries at least once a week. After all, she couldn't reject the food once it appeared in her icebox, or it'd go to waste.

The first time she saw the fresh vegetables and lovely cuts of meat she frowned at him.

"You shouldn't have done that," she said.

"Maybe it was the *domaći*," he said with a grin. His mother used to read him stories about the *domaći*, the little fairy creatures who lived in a person's kitchen cupboards and did good deeds for their host. They seemed like a good explanation for the bountiful food in her fridge.

CHAPTER FIFTEEN

The frown melted and Ema returned his smile. "*Domaći*, eh? That brings me back. Well, if you happen to see the little creatures, please thank them for me. The gifts are appreciated."

"I will," he replied.

"You're a good boy," she said. "You should find a nice girl and get married."

Frank immediately thought of the beauty he'd met that day long ago. Ljubica. Those brown eyes with the golden flecks. He longed to touch her creamy skin and pull her into his embrace. He blushed thinking of what it might be like to kiss her.

"Ah, so you do have someone," Ema said.

Frank sighed and shook his head. "No. I mean, yes, but she's back home. Back in Yugoslavia."

He told her all about that day in the park, describing Ljubica in great detail. He realized that Ljubica was the only girl for him. He was in love.

"So, you only saw her that one day?" Ema asked. "A year ago?"

"Yes. But that was enough. She stole my heart."

Ema's eyes sparkled. "How beautiful."

They fell silent, both lost in thought. Finally Frank said, "I'll write her. Today. I'll tell her to find a lawyer and come to me."

Ema beamed at him. "Yes, do that. How can she resist such romance?"

Ema helped him pick out a card from her collection. He wrote a passionate plea to Ljubica and sent the card that day to his love's uncle's address. He was happy that he'd insisted that she give him that address before they parted last year.

With Ema's permission, he'd given Ljubica Ema's address so that they might correspond. Frank waited and waited for her to reply. When the slim envelope finally arrived, Ema handed it to him. Frank's hands shook as he opened the letter and quickly scanned it for her answer.

No. The answer was no.

Frank looked up at Ema, as his hand holding the light blue letter dropped to his side. His head felt as if it was made of lead as it dropped to his chest, and his shoulders slumped as he studied the wooden floor. Numbness threatened to take over his mind and body. Grief tore at his heart as he struggled to keep his emotions in check.

Ema touched his shoulder and gave him a look of empathy. "I'm sorry. However, no might not be final."

Grasping at any hope she offered, he looked up into her warm eyes. "What do you mean?"

"Well, 'no' might mean 'not right now.' What did she say, precisely?"

Frank picked up the letter and read it out loud. Ljubica said she couldn't risk leaving. It was too dangerous. And she had only completed the academic requirements for high school. "It says here that she's enrolling in a government program called Radnia Akcija."

"What is that?" Ema asked.

He continued to read. "It sounds like a typical communist work program. She's required to do a certain amount of volunteer work before she can get her high school diploma."

"What kind of work will she do?"

Frank looked down at the letter, then said, "Teaching. She wants to be a schoolteacher."

"So, see? She just wants to finish up her education and get the diploma. That's logical."

"But it's not like she promises to join me after. She just said no."

Ema smiled and patted his arm. "She needs a little more security. You're suggesting that she leave everything she knows:

CHAPTER FIFTEEN

her friends, her school, her chance to work as a teacher, and any remaining family she has there."

"She lost her parents," Frank said. "She does have a few aunts and uncles, but from what I can tell, the one nasty aunt just works her all the time. When Ljubica would come to visit from the orphanage, the aunt would put her to work for the weekend."

"Poor girl."

"She has nothing to leave behind," Frank said, feeling a budding anger growing within him. "I can offer her a lot more."

"But she doesn't *know* that," Ema said gently. "She's scared to leave what she knows."

Frank crossed his arms across his chest. "Maybe."

"Wait until you get settled. Find work, then write her again. Tell her all about the good things. Send her a little spending money. Show her you plan to take care of her. Show her that you'll spoil her and love her. Then she'll join you."

Frank nodded slowly. "That could work."

"Just don't complain about anything. And give her some time to think it over. She's saying no now, but notice she isn't saying there is anyone else. She's still single. If she truly wasn't interested, she would have mentioned a boyfriend or fiancé."

Frank relaxed a bit and allowed a smile to form on his lips. "That's true."

Following Ema's advice, he didn't write to Ljubica again. He wanted to, and picked up a pen a few times, but then he put it down and walked away. Ema was right. The last thing he wanted to do was to scare her away.

* * *

Frank nearly skipped on his way home. It was late Thursday and the next day was Day of the Austrian Flag, a new Austrian holiday celebrating the country's independence after World War II. Ema had explained that this day commemorated the adoption of an important federal constitutional law the previous year. The new law proclaimed the country's permanent neutrality, swearing that they would never join another suppressive military regime or allow them to set up base in Austria again.

With every passing day, Frank was more and more grateful that he was in this free country. Getting an extra day off to celebrate what made Austria truly great, gave him a feeling of well-being and contentment.

On top of that, the Hungarian Revolution had kicked off just a few days prior. Frank rejoiced that he could receive reliable updates on a regular basis. This was so different from the state-controlled news sources of Yugoslavia. While he hadn't learned enough German to understand the news reports on the radio and in the Austrian newspapers, he hungrily read the small, Croatian paper that Ema received.

The world was changing before his eyes, and Frank wasn't just a silent observer. He was a full-fledged participant. He walked tall knowing that he had risked all to escape the suppression of Tito and now could celebrate with likeminded people freely in this new country. He was a part of the rebellion against communism and tyranny.

He was whistling a little tune that Mr. Gruber had been humming earlier that day as he walked through the front door. Ema gave him a huge smile and handed him a slim blue envelope.

Picking it up, he burst out into a joyous cheer. "Another letter from home!" Frank said.

The only raincloud on his perfectly executed escape was that he had no way to see his family. He wondered how they all were. He wished he could tease little Mila to make her screech in outrage, then giggle over the silliness of it. She was

CHAPTER FIFTEEN

such an adorable younger sister. And how he longed to fall into the embrace of his mother and breathe in her wonderful scent of spices and whatever she was cooking that day. There was no hug like *Majka's*.

However, most of all he missed visiting his father in the hospital. He had been his father's only link to close family. Since he was stuck in the hospital in Zagreb, far from home, he rarely received any visitors. If he was lucky, he'd see Josip or his wife once a month. So Frank's time with his father was precious to both of them.

Frank sat on the couch and carefully opened the thin paper. Ema went to the kitchen to pour him a cup of coffee. When she returned with it, he had the letter ready to read.

"Thank you," he said.

She smiled and patted his head. "Enjoy your letter. I'll be in the kitchen making dinner."

He took a sip of coffee, set it down, and then leaned back to read the treasure in his hand. After he read the first line, though, his smile vanished. Anguish ripped through him.

His father had passed. Alone. No one had been there to hold his hand or say any final words. By the time his mother and siblings had learned that he'd taken a turn for the worse, it had been too late.

The words of the letter blurred, and he couldn't read the rest. He set it aside and reached for the coffee cup. His hands trembled too much to pick it up, though, so he just slumped back. After a few moments he picked the letter up and read on.

No one blamed him. That was something. However, he couldn't escape the gnawing feeling that he should have been there.

"What's wrong?" Ema cried from the doorway.

Woodenly, Frank looked up at her. "My father died of cancer last week." He couldn't bring himself to say anything else, as he was sure to dissolve into a torrent of unwanted tears.

Ema immediately walked over and sat on the couch next to Frank. She pulled him into her arms and cooed an understanding of his grief. As if her kindness and understanding gave him permission to weep, Frank's tears began to fall, moistening the flower print dress covering her shoulder.

"I didn't know your father well, but I know your mother loved him. She wrote to me often about his lovely brown eyes when he was courting her. Then later, she confided in me how lucky she felt to have made a true love match. While many of her friends married people they could barely stand because their parents wished it, she had been allowed to follow her heart."

All Frank could do was nod. His parents had been in love. There had been a lot of laughter as well as animated discussions growing up. It had been a lively childhood. Yes, his parents had argued, but never had it pushed past the point of mutual respect.

And now his father was gone. Forever.

A new wave of tears fell as Frank considered his *Majka*. She must be devasted. Of course, it had been a half a year since Ivan had moved to Zagreb to get the best care Yugoslavia could offer. She'd become used to being without her husband.

Still, he wished he could be there for his mother. Guilt washed over him as he realized that she'd lost her husband and one of her sons in the same year. In previous letters, she'd asked who was cooking for him now. When Frank had reassured her that Ema was taking good care of him, *Majka* had written of her approval. It was one point of comfort he could offer his mother.

Chapter Sixteen

As winter approached, Frank realized he couldn't stay in Austria much longer. He loved this country but was constantly reminded that he was a refugee by the officials he would check in with every week.

"Unfortunately, Austria can't keep everyone who crosses the border," the immigration officer explained. "We wish we could."

There were too many desperate people crossing every day, especially after the dismal failure of the Hungarian Revolution. More and more young people were hurtling themselves across the border any way they could.

"So, it says here," the man said, opening up Frank's file, "you want to go to Australia. Fine place."

Frank shook his head. "No, I changed my mind."

"Oh?"

"Can I go to Canada?"

The man nodded slowly. "Yes, they have opened their borders to the Hungarians and others fleeing oppression. Like you."

"How many have gone there?"

The man leaned back in his chair and stretched. "Oh, that's hard to say, but it's in the thousands by now. Based on various reports, I'd hazard to guess it to be around three or four thousand."

"And there's many more that still need a home," Frank said.

"Many more," the officer said with a nod. "When all is said and done, Canada will probably have tens of thousands of new residents."

"Where could I go?"

"Winnipeg. You know, I read somewhere…" the man said, pausing as he sifted through papers on his desk. Picking up one, he read it for a moment, then nodded. "Yes, this says that they're paying money for anyone immigrating to Winnipeg."

"Really?" Frank said sitting forward in his chair. "That's great. How much?"

"Fifteen dollars a week."

Frank whistled low. That was a lot of money for doing nothing but living in a place. "Sign me up!"

The man nodded. "Done. There's a ship leaving in a little over a month from Bremen, Germany."

As Frank filled out the paperwork, he asked, "How will I get to the port?"

The man picked up the piece of paper again and nodded. "There's a train. We'll cover the expense. It leaves the day before and will take about fifteen hours."

By the time Frank left the small office, his head was spinning. There was so much to take in. He began to wonder how he'd like Canada. It would be so different from any place he had ever lived. Although life in Austria was different, it was close to the only place he'd ever called home.

Home.

That was a strange word. What was home?

Once, it had been his family farm. Then it was the burgeoning city of Zagreb. Now it was on the floor in Ema's apartment.

What was next?

Well, he'd have to wait and see.

CHAPTER SIXTEEN

* * *

Frank carried his suitcase onto the enormous ocean liner that would be his home for the next week. The bag had been given to him by the officials, but since he only had one extra set of clothes and a toothbrush, it was as light as a feather. Still, he was happy to have the bag. After all, no one could tell that he carried so little and owned nothing.

That will change one day.

The large gray ship was like something out of a movie—elegant and luxurious. In talking to others at the immigration camp, he'd heard that most refugees had to make do with ships that were refitted for passengers, sleeping in large rooms crammed with forty or more people. That certainly wasn't the case for him.

Frank had to share his cabin with only three other men. He felt fortunate that he'd gotten to it first so he could select a top bunk. He hoped he wouldn't vomit on his bunkmate's head in the middle of the night, but he couldn't make any promises. Motion sickness had always been a problem for him, ever since he was a kid.

Back on deck, he looked out at the harbor of Bremen, Germany, and watched the crew scurry around, untying large ropes and making ready to depart. The dock was filled with people waving up at the passengers. He felt as though he were a part of an historic voyage.

Frank glanced over at a young girl who appeared to be in her early twenties. She was pretty, but not as beautiful as Ljubica. The girl waved at a middle-aged couple on the dock, probably her parents. The woman was dabbing her eyes with a handkerchief.

He immediately thought of Ema and their tearful good-bye. She'd clung to him with such ferocity that he wondered if she would ever let go. Frank was excited to start his new life but was sad to leave the only family he had in the free world.

A month before he left, he'd written to *Majka* telling her of his plans and promising to send an address where she could send letters as soon as he was settled. She wrote back with the name and address of an old family friend, Lanka, who lived in Toronto.

Frank had looked on the map and saw that Toronto was two thousand kilometers from where he'd land in Winnipeg. Might as well have a contact in Brazil for all that it would help him.

Ema had agreed to forward any mail he might receive, once he was settled. His heart fluttered as he wondered if Ljubica might write to him. It had been months since he'd received that one letter from her.

Don't forget me.

The gray clouds parted just as the tugboat arrived to assist the ocean liner from the port. It didn't take long before the ship was free of the smaller boat and moving on its own. Frank stood on the deck until dinner and watched the shoreline on the port side fade out of sight.

The dining room was on one of the lowest decks. The seats were bolted to the floor, but they swiveled, which made eating a challenge. There were no windows in the large room, and it didn't take long before Frank felt queasy. Still, he was starved, so he took many deep breaths as he gulped down the chicken, vegetables, and rice. He wished he could have enjoyed the delicious food more; the chef was talented. However, he knew if he stayed much longer, he would embarrass himself by throwing up the contents of his stomach.

Racing back up to the deck, he stood at the rail and watched the waves bob up and down. It was dark, but he could make out the horizon, and the fresh air helped calm his stomach.

CHAPTER SIXTEEN

He spent a few hours on the deck. Feeling better, he headed to his cabin, where he stumbled up onto his bunk, nodding a greeting to his cabinmates. He was exhausted and managed to fall asleep despite the rolling motion of the ship.

Frank awoke before the sun came up. His stomach rebelled against the surging of the ship, and he quickly climbed down from his bunk and went out to the corridor. He was tossed back and forth against the walls, then retched the contents of his stomach onto the floor. Moaning, he crawled to the stairs, then picked himself up to a standing position using the banister to aid him. He climbed up slowly to the upper level.

Large waves crashed over the railings, drenching the deck as sheets of rain fell. He longed to go outside and feel the fresh air on his face but knew he couldn't hold onto the rail as he had the night before. The sea and the weather were too rough.

All he could do was fall to the ground near the doorway and moan. It was better than his room, but not by much.

By mid-afternoon the storm had subsided, and the sun made an appearance. Frank pulled himself up and pushed open the door, staggering over to the railing. He gulped the cool ocean air and hoped the weather would stay calm. It was tolerable if he could remain outside. However, he knew he couldn't. He'd need to sleep.

An officer came around the next day and gave all the refugees a coupon for two dollars which could be spent on the ship. Frank stared at the gift, then said, "Thank you!"

He rushed to the drugstore and purchased some anti-nausea medication with the money. It knocked him out, which was fine with him as he sorely needed uninterrupted sleep.

His three cabinmates were not faring any better than he was, and when the drug store ran out of the medication, he shared his supply with them. Unfortunately, that meant he ran out before they reached their destination. The last few days were unbearable as a new storm hit and they all fell victim to its effects.

By the time Frank arrived at the port of Halifax, he was eager to disembark. All of the refugees received travel documents, along with a temporary Canadian identification card. As Frank walked down the gangplank, his legs shook from the ordeal of the ocean crossing. He'd barely been able to keep anything down for the last few days. When he and the others were processed through the Welcome Center, they were given a hot meal. Frank hungrily devoured the food. He was also given a new set of clothes.

Something to put in this nearly empty suitcase.

Then everyone was given a medical exam. Frank worried about the results since he knew he looked pale from the voyage. Fortunately the doctors recognized the symptoms of seasickness and determined that he didn't carry any viruses.

Before Frank knew it, he was on a train heading for Toronto. It would take nearly a full day to reach the city. Then he'd be off to Winnipeg. He still felt shaky from his time on the ship, but the gentle rocking of the train was preferable to the heaving of the ship.

Looking around, he saw that most of the people in the compartment were Hungarian. Although he could only understand a few words, he recognized the distinct language. Frank smiled thinking about how all these men and women had managed to escape the suppressive Soviet-installed government. He wondered how many had fought in the short-lived revolution that had ended so dismally.

Frank needed to stretch his legs, so he walked the length of a few train cars, nodding at passengers that he passed. They smiled at him. Images of sullen and drawn faces looking away on the trains of Yugoslavia popped into his mind. Everyone was so much happier here than back home. Such a difference.

CHAPTER SIXTEEN

Suddenly he stopped. His ears picked up a few familiar words from the other end of the train car. He stiffened and scanned the area. There were three men standing by the door chatting. From that distance he couldn't make out full sentences, but he was sure they were speaking Croatian.

Grinning, he walked over to them and learned they had been students in Zagreb. They were just as eager to see him as he was them, and they all exchanged names.

"Where are you going?" Frank asked the man who'd introduced himself as Jakov.

"Toronto," they all said in unison.

Frank nodded.

"And you?" Jakov asked.

"Winnipeg."

All three winced. Then Jakov said, "Any way to change that?"

Alarm shot through Frank's frame. "Why?" he whispered. It was clear they knew something he didn't.

"Didn't you research the place?" Jakov asked.

Frank shook his head. "No. Why should I have?"

"It's freezing cold six months of the year," the one named Daniel said.

"How cold?" Frank asked.

Jakov shrugged. "Below zero."

"*Way* below zero," Daniel said. "Like minus ten or twenty."

"I heard the record low was something like minus forty-five," the third one said.

"People get frostbite and lose a foot when they're out in weather like that for more than a few minutes," Daniel added.

Frank's mind reeled with this new information. How could he have been so daft as to not do research about the area he was committing to live in for the rest of his life? Losing a foot to frostbite wasn't part of his plans for making his mark on this world and becoming a wealthy man. Besides, if people couldn't go outside, they couldn't visit his shoe shop and buy from him. All of his sacrifices and risks would have been for nothing. And he knew that Ljubica would never follow him to such an unpleasant place.

"I won't survive that," Frank said.

"Don't worry," Jakov said. "The officials will probably let you stay in Toronto."

Toronto would be much better. He smiled suddenly as he remembered *Majka's* letter. Lanka. He'd have a connection there. She might be able to take him in.

"It's an idea," Frank said. "I wonder what kind of story I can come up with."

"Well I saw you on the ship. You were mighty sick," Jakov said.

Frank blushed. It was so embarrassing. "Yeah."

"Tell them that you're still not quite recovered, and you'd just like to stay put," Jakov said. "Chances are, they'll let you."

Frank nodded. He thanked the trio and went back to his seat. He had a lot to think about, but soon the thoughts turned into dreams as his head lolled against the window.

Chapter Seventeen

When the train stopped in Toronto, Frank got off. His ticket was for Winnipeg, but he didn't want to continue on to that frozen place. He stepped onto the platform and nearly choked from the frozen air.
What time was it?
He looked around and found a large clock. It was almost midnight. Everything would be closed. He followed the crush of people into the warm train station and took a seat on a bench. Although he'd slept a lot of the way to Toronto, he still felt exhausted.
He fingered his mother's letter in his pocket. He couldn't approach this stranger, this friend of his *Majka* in the middle of the night in the freezing cold weather. She'd most likely be frightened. Then where would he be?
As he sat on the bench, he heard a host of languages pass him. French, German, Hungarian, but nothing was familiar to his ears. He closed his eyes and let the noise wash over him. He wished he had thought to sit near Jakov and the others. Maybe they'd be able to help him.
Suddenly his eyes snapped open as he heard two male voices talking about work in Croatian. He stood up and scanned the area. He quickly spotted two young men a few meters away, chatting amiably.
Frank smoothed his hair with his hand, knowing it probably was a mess. He approached the men, cleared his throat,

and said with a broad smile, "Hello! I couldn't help but notice that you're Croats."

The two stopped talking, returned his smile, and introduced themselves. Frank was happy that they knew where Mali Bukovec was. It turned out they were cousins from Dubrovnik: Josip and Zoran.

Frank gave a quick synopsis of his story and finished by saying, "I have a huge favor to ask…"

"Of course, you can come with us," Zoran said. "What kind of people would we be if we left you in this train station alone in the middle of the night? Croats don't do that. Not to fellow Croats."

Josip nodded. "Absolutely. Come home with us. Tomorrow we'll show you where the Immigration Office is." He reached for Frank's suitcase. "Let me help you with that."

"Oh, no," Frank said. "Don't worry about it."

"Don't be silly," Josip said. He pulled the bag from Frank's hand, and it flew up high into the air. He laughed. "Look, Zoran, another rich one! What you got in here?"

Frank blushed. "Everything I own. You know, a set of clothes, a toothbrush…" He let his voice trail off.

"Don't worry," Zoran said, punching his cousin in the arm. "We all started out that way."

Frank grinned. "Mark my words, though. I won't be this poor for long!"

* * *

The next morning, Frank left the cramped apartment with his suitcase and thanked the cousins for hosting him.

"Come back if you need to spend another night," Josip said.

"I will," he promised.

The sun shone brightly in the sky, but the wind was cold as Frank made his way to the Immigration Office. Walking

CHAPTER SEVENTEEN

into the building, he enjoyed the warmth of the large open room. He was quickly ushered into the private office of an official who spoke decent Croatian. He was a portly man with hair that he combed over to hide an obvious bald spot. Frank looked away, not wanting to be rude.

As the man collected the paperwork he needed, Frank suddenly realized he hadn't thought up a good story to explain why he wanted to stay in Toronto. Should he mention that he was supposed to go to Winnipeg? Probably not. Most likely this official would want to see the plan out to the end and wouldn't allow him to stay.

"My name is Oliver Matich," the officer said, breaking into Frank's thoughts. "I'm here to help you get settled in Canada. What is your name?"

"Frank Katana."

The first dozen questions were easy. Then came the question he had been dreading.

"Destination?"

"Could I stay here?" Frank asked. He gave the man a pleading look that he accented with a smile.

Mr. Matich squinted. "Didn't they *give* you a destination city when they approved your application to come to Canada?"

Frank just stared at him. He again wondered what the best course of action would be. Honesty was the easier option, as it required no calculation. Nor would he need to memorize any lies told. However, fear shot through him every time he considered how his toes could freeze off in Winnipeg.

"They gave me a choice," Frank said, slowly.

That wasn't completely a lie. He had been given a choice and he'd chosen fifteen dollars a week, not knowing anything else. At the time, that sounded great. Now, he knew better.

"I'd like to stay here in Toronto," he continued. He paused as he gauged the man's expression. It was hard to read. "I mean, if that's all right with you. I had a rough trip across the ocean. Sea travel didn't sit well with me. I'd prefer to just stay put."

Mr. Matich nodded slowly. "Let me see what I can do." He shuffled through more papers and pulled out a new form. "May I see your passport?"

Frank pulled it out and handed it to him. "The birthday's wrong on there."

"Is it? That's odd," Mr. Matich said with a frown.

"Yeah, I'm not sure why, but when they gave it to me in Austria, it said I was born on January 31st, but I was born on the 29th."

The man's face scrunched up in confusion. "Well, what does your birth certificate say?"

"I don't know. I lost it."

Mr. Matich stared at the passport for a moment, before lifting his eyes to Frank. "I recommend that you just keep it the 31st. It's less confusing that way. You can celebrate it on whichever day you like, but it's best to keep it simple. Agreed?"

Frank nodded. Then he cleared his throat. "I heard that sometimes the government will give new immigrants a little money to get started."

The man shook his head. "That's only if you're willing to go to a less popular city. If you went to Winnipeg, for instance, I could get you that deal. Are you interested in going there?"

Frank shook his head vehemently. "No."

Mr. Matich smiled. "I don't blame you. It's not pleasant in the winter. Toronto's a good city. You'll like it here."

"Can you help me find a job?"

The man shuffled through a few papers, shaking his head, then got up and went to his filing cabinet. He rummaged through it for a few moments and said, "Ah, here's something!" He pulled out a tattered piece of paper and brought it to his desk, leaving the filing cabinet open. He copied information onto another slip of paper and handed it to Frank.

CHAPTER SEVENTEEN

"A local mattress company is looking for three or four men to stuff springs into mattresses. No experience required," he said.

"Thank you," Frank said, feeling a rush of relief.

The man nodded, then said, "Do you have a place to live?"

"No, but I know someone in Toronto."

"Oh, who?"

"Lanka."

"Last name?"

Frank reached into his pocket but couldn't find the letter from his mother. He stood up and patted all of his pockets, front and back. It had been there just yesterday. Had it fallen out? For the life of him, he couldn't remember the last name of his distant relative.

"I don't know," he said quietly.

"Where does this Lanka live?"

Frank turned red as he studied the floor. "It looks like I lost the letter. I'll have to find out. I don't know Lanka, but hoped to contact her when I arrived, after I settled."

The man nodded. "Well, in the meantime..." he said, taking back the slip of paper. He jotted down another note and handed it back. "You can go to this Croatian church. Someone there will probably help you." He gave Frank directions.

"What do I do if no one can give me a place to stay?" Frank asked.

Mr. Matich gave him a look of pity. "Someone will help you. They're good people."

Chapter Eighteen

It didn't take Frank long to figure out how to navigate his way through the streets of Toronto. He marveled at the streetcars filled with people traveling up and down the wide streets. Brick buildings towered over him, making him feel like a little ant in a great city, alone without family and friends. Although the weather was cold, the sun was still shining brightly. He was grateful for that. Gripping his suitcase, he wondered where he'd land that night.

Passersby greeted him with a smile, putting him at ease. He returned their smiles with one of his own, which naturally put him in a better mood. As he passed a little old man sweeping outside his shop, Frank tipped his woolen cap and greeted him in Croatian. Although the man wouldn't understand the words, Frank knew he'd appreciate the gesture.

The shopkeeper motioned for him to wait a moment, then returned with a piece of fruit Frank had never seen before. It was an orange sphere, bright and inviting.

What a strange sort of apple, he thought.

Frank bowed in gratitude and the man grinned at him, while motioning him to eat the fruit.

Frank smiled and bit into it. The skin didn't give like a normal apple, so he gave the man another look and put more strength into the bite. The intensely bitter flavor made him grimace, but he didn't want to offend the man, so he chewed the fruit and did his best to refrain from spitting out the awful rind.

CHAPTER EIGHTEEN

The shopkeeper frowned briefly and hurried away, leaving Frank to wonder if he offended him. It was a gift, after all. A gift of food for a hungry man. However, Frank thought he'd be ill if he continued to eat it, so he tossed the offending fruit into the nearest receptacle and hoped he'd never be offered another again.

When he arrived at the church, Frank discovered it was a gymnasium converted into a Catholic church. He tried the doors, but they were locked, so he sat on the stoop and waited until noon, when a hunched man in a long overcoat came to open the building up.

Fortunately, the clergyman, who introduced himself as Reverend Jure, spoke enough Croatian to invite him in from the cold. Frank entered a large room in which folding chairs were set up. It wasn't much warmer than outside, but when the man brought him a hot cup of tea, Frank felt better. Then Reverend Jure brought him a few sugar cookies wrapped in a small cloth napkin to quiet his grumbling tummy. They were sweet and tasty and quickly gone.

An hour later a few more people came in. Two elderly women sat together at one end of the room in prayer, while a middle-aged man wearing a large woolen scarf around his neck went to speak to Reverend Jure.

Before long, the two men walked over to Frank. Reverend Jure introduced him to the other man, David. They spoke another language, English perhaps; Frank wasn't sure.

When they'd finished, Reverend Jure said, "Go with David. He stay for night and next."

Frank cocked his head to the right and deciphered the words. Frank folded his hands together and put his head against them as if sleeping and then asked, "Is he going to let me stay with him?"

Reverend Jure nodded and smiled. "Yes."

Frank shook hands with David. "Thank you!"

When David smiled in response, Frank noticed he was missing a number of teeth. David motioned for Frank to follow him, so he did, waving farewell to Reverend Jure.

David walked quickly through various alleyways until he reached a small apartment complex. He fiddled with his keys, then opened the front door. He turned back to Frank and motioned for him to follow him up the narrow wooden steps. Finally, when they reached the third floor, David grasped another key and put it into the lock, turning it.

When the door opened, David motioned for Frank to enter. It was one of the smallest apartments Frank had ever seen. It was clear this poor man could hardly afford to support himself, let alone take care of another. Frank instantly felt guilty but put a smile on his face and bowed to the man saying "Thank you" in English. It was one of the few phrases he'd picked up, but a worthwhile one. This man deserved his gratitude.

Frank pulled out the slip of paper he'd received from the immigration officer. He pointed at the address of the possible job. "Do you know where this is?" If he could start working, he could save money so he could move out and be less of a burden to this nice man.

The man studied the paper, then smiled. "Yes," he replied, then said a lot of things that Frank didn't understand.

Frank shook his head and splayed his hands out in front of himself to communicate that he didn't understand a word the man was saying. "I'm so sorry, but I don't understand English. Yet."

David stopped talking and nodded, patting Frank on the shoulder. He imagined the man probably said something to the effect of "don't worry about it," but he couldn't be sure. One thing was certain, Frank had to learn the language if he was going to survive, let alone excel in Canada. One of his first purchases would be a dictionary.

CHAPTER EIGHTEEN

David motioned for Frank to follow him over to the corner of the studio apartment. There he had stored a few cans of food. He opened one and handed it to Frank, giving him a fork.

Frank nodded his thanks and took a bite, thinking it was tuna fish. However, he nearly gagged on the mystery meat. With great difficulty he swallowed the bite before putting the can down. David didn't seem to notice, as he was devouring his can with gusto.

Frank turned the can around and saw a picture of a cat on the label. That explained it. This was a feast fit for a feline, just not a man.

After David finished his can, he picked up Frank's and looked questioningly at him. Frank motioned that he wasn't hungry. Although he'd only had three small cookies and was starving, he couldn't stomach eating another bite of cat food.

David shrugged and made quick work of the can, licking it clean before tossing the empty container into the trash.

After, David motioned for Frank to follow him out the door and down the stairs. Frank realized he was going to take him to the mattress shop, so he made a mental note of the path the man was walking. Every now and then he'd call out to David to slow down so he could get his bearings. The journey was mostly on a main road, St. Clair. Since it was just after noon, the streets were bustling with people on a lunch break. Frank envied them. He saw a few workers by the side of the road enjoying a variety of beverages. He licked his lips as he imagined what it would be like for him to sip on juice or Coca-Cola.

It took them about an hour and a half to arrive at the address on the slip of paper. David didn't seem bothered by the walk, but Frank realized he'd need to take a streetcar to and from this location or he'd lose most of the day. Besides, the long walk would be exhausting each day.

When they arrived at the mattress store, David pointed to a sign taped to the front window that bore two large words that Frank couldn't make out. When David pointed to Frank and gave him a thumbs up, Frank realized the sign probably said that they were still looking for workers.

Well that was something.

Frank went in and David followed. He realized that David was probably interested in the job, too. He hoped there were still two positions open.

A large beefy man came out from the back room and sized up Frank and David, then grunted.

"Do you speak Croatian?" Frank asked hopefully.

When the man looked at him in confusion, Frank sighed. No luck.

David spoke to the man, who nodded.

As they continued to speak to each other, a thin man with a pencil mustache said from the corner "I speak a little Croatian. May I be of service?"

Frank gave a cry of delight. "Could you please tell him that I'm here for the job?"

"Of course," he said. "I'm Liam. I am a customer. This is Miles. He's the owner of this shop."

Liam waited for Miles and David to stop speaking, then turned to Miles and rapidly spoke in English. After a few minutes, Liam turned back to Frank. "It pays sixty cents per hour, and you can start now, if you'd like."

Frank gulped. *Sixty cents per hour?* How could he live off that?

Chapter Nineteen

The work at the mattress factory was dismal. Every muscle in Frank's body hurt, and his hands were bloody with blisters. Sixty cents an hour. There had to be an easier way to earn a living. He looked down at his arms and grimaced at the burns from the hot glue that decorated his forearms.

If I have to keep this up much longer, I'm going to die.

Although he was tempted to quit more than once, Frank stuck it out for the week. At least the streetcar made the journey there much easier. However, it cost ten cents, so the ride to and from work each day cost him nearly half an hour of work. He had to come up with a new plan.

When Saturday came, Frank was relieved to have two days off. He decided to use the time to find another job. There had to be something in shoe repair or manufacturing in this large city.

He walked around the neighborhood near the small apartment. He couldn't bear to be cooped up all day in that place, which smelled like the inside of a dumpster. He was grateful to his host, but the man had no sense of personal hygiene.

As Frank turned onto Ossington Street, he noticed a small shoe store with a similar sign in the window that the mattress store had when he'd first approached it. Using his newly purchased pocket Croatian-to-English dictionary, he'd learned that the words on the sign indeed advertised for workers.

Frank walked into the shop, and the small bell on the door announced his presence. The front of the shop was empty of people. Dust covered every surface, and the floor was littered with the remains of receipts and dirty napkins. As he walked to the register, he jumped as something touched his foot. Looking down, he noticed a small mouse scurry behind the counter. Frank stood patiently waiting for the owner to come to greet him. After a few minutes, he walked around the counter and poked his head through the open door to the back of the establishment.

Sitting in a wooden chair, his head lolled back, was a man with a scruffy salt-and-pepper beard. His desk was piled high with a dozen or so shoes in various stages of repair. Looking around the small backroom, he saw dusty shelves filled with a number of other shoes.

Frank cleared his throat and waited. Nothing. He tried again. All he could hear were the snores coming from the man. He debated what to do. Although he felt uncomfortable disturbing the man, he could see that the cobbler needed assistance with the repairs. Frank was itching to get his hands on a few of these shoes. Their owners must be eager to get them back.

"Mister?" he called out quietly. Then again, with a little more force, "Mister?"

Frank waited, then took a few steps forward. His nose wrinkled at the smell of dead fish and alcohol coming from the form in front of him. If it wasn't for the steady snores, Frank would have wondered if the man was even alive. Frank called out to the man again, but still got no response. Finally, he touched the man's shoulder. That had the desired effect.

The man's eyes popped open, and he sat up. Without looking at Frank he grunted. He then muttered something incomprehensible in English.

"I-I'm sorry," Frank said in Croatian. His English still wasn't strong enough to speak yet, but he was studying the dictionary every day.

CHAPTER NINETEEN

The man stood and looked at Frank. His expression immediately softened as he looked Frank up and down. Then he said slowly in Croatian, "Ah, you from Yugoslavia. I'm Jan Peder. I speak a little." He flashed Frank a broad smile.

Frank nodded and introduced himself. Not able to place the man's accent, he asked, "Where are you from, Mr. Peder?"

"Ukraine," he said, his voice taking on a silky texture. "And it's Jan."

"Well, Jan," Frank said. "I trained for many years as a cobbler. I earned a master diploma in Zagreb."

"Are you looking for work?"

"Yes, sir, I am."

Jan reached out a hand and gently stroked Frank's arm before squeezing his muscle slightly. "That is wonderful. I need help."

Frank pulled away from the man's touch. "How much does the position pay?"

If he wasn't so desperate, he would have left the dirty backroom, but he needed employment and couldn't stand the thought of returning to the mattress shop for another week.

Frank thought that he probably would take the job even if it paid less than his current job, but he hoped it would pay more. If he could just make enough, he could try to find Lanka in the hopes that he could move in with her. When he realized he'd lost her address, he'd telegrammed home and his mother had sent it to him again. However, he didn't want to reach out to Lanka until he had secured real employment.

The man put his hand on his chin. "That's a good question," he said, then paused for a moment, lost in thought.

Frank waited for him to continue. As the moments ticked by, it puzzled him that the cobbler didn't have a ready answer. After all, he had a sign advertising for help.

Finally, Frank cleared his throat and said, "Yes?"

The man looked startled and nodded. "One dollar and thirty cents?"

Frank's mouth dropped open. "An hour?"

The man nodded. "Sure," he said, giving Frank a wink. "Why not?"

This was the strangest encounter Frank had ever had. However, he was thrilled by the pay. He could put up with the strange man for one dollar and thirty cents per hour. Frank took the man's hand and shook it vehemently. "That would be great. Thank you!"

As they shook, the man placed his other hand on top of their hands, and Frank felt the man's thumb gently stroking his palm. Frank sorely wanted to pull away from the handshake, but he didn't want the man to change his mind. He could put up with it for one thirty.

"When do I start?" Frank asked with a nervous grin.

"How's now? Jan said, releasing his grip.

Frank relaxed and smiled. "I can do that." He didn't need the day off.

* * *

The next day, Frank walked a kilometer across town and found the address his mother had sent him. It surprised Frank that Jan opened his shop on Sunday, as most businesses were closed. However, when Frank explained the situation, he had been allowed to leave midday. Frank was aware that no repairs would happen while he was gone, so he'd have to show up an hour early the next morning. That was fine, though. He now had a decent income and could afford to pay Lanka.

He smiled as he picked up the pace. He could also write to Ljubica and entreat her again to consider joining him. He

CHAPTER NINETEEN

could only imagine what she'd say when he wrote her that he was now making one dollar thirty an hour.

When Frank found Lanka's street, he looked around the neighborhood and relaxed. The tall, brick duplexes were close together but looked to be in good repair. It was much better than where he'd been staying with David.

Finding the correct house, he climbed the five steps and knocked on the door. No one answered. *Damn*. He'd hoped she'd be home on a Sunday. Frank rubbed his hands to warm them and leaned against the wall to wait.

An hour later, a woman in a bulky coat strode up the front path. She was looking down and only raised her head when she came to the steps. She saw Frank and stopped short. Looking a little frightened, she pulled her coat closer together and said in English, "Who are you?"

Frank smiled and said in Croatian, "I'm Frank Katana, Stefanija's son. From Mali Bukovec."

Lanka's cold expression seemed to melt before his eyes. The elderly woman raced up the stairs to give him a hug. "Your mother wrote me that you might be coming. Come in, come in. I'm sorry I was late." She inserted the key into the lock and continued, "I work for a seamstress in town. She had a last-minute job she needed finished. A wedding later today."

Lanka opened the door and shuffled in. Frank followed, and when she turned on the light, he saw that the small home was decorated with many handmade objects that hung from the walls and sat on various shelves. Dozens of hoops holding embroidered pieces, little teddy bears and dolls, as well as other crafts, adorned the place.

"Did you make all of these?" Frank asked in wonder as he studied a framed cross-stitch pattern of two hummingbirds hovering around a tall purple flower.

Lanka blushed. "Yes, it's what I love to do."

"I can tell. I feel the same about shoes."

"Yes, Stefanija told me that you were a master cobbler. That's a good business."

Frank turned to her. "I just found a new job with a local cobbler."

"Congratulations!" she said. "I'm so glad."

"I was wondering…" he began, then realized it was probably too soon to ask if he could live with her. She didn't know him at all.

Lanka tilted her head. "Would you like to stay with me?"

Frank felt a rush of relief and grinned. "Yes, yes, I would. Thank you! Do you have a spare room?"

"No, but you can sleep in the living room here. I keep to my room at night, so you'll have privacy."

Frank nodded and tried to hide his disappointment. One day he'd be able to afford a real room in a house. However, that seemed like such a luxury now. "What's the rent?"

Lanka waved a hand in front of her. "Whatever you can afford will be fine. I just could use some help with the costs. I don't quite make enough with the job, so I've had to take on some laundry to supplement."

It was then that Frank noticed the bundles sitting neatly on the couch. "I'll give you whatever I can," he said.

* * *

Friday morning, Frank came to the shoe shop just before sunrise and unlocked the door. Jan had grumbled when he had requested a key, but the alternative was not workable. His employer preferred to arrive just before lunch, which explained why he was so behind on all of his orders.

Frank had managed to make the needed repairs on a few dozen of the backlogged work orders that filled the shelves. Although those customers were now happy, he'd hardly made a dent in the mountain of work. If he truly wanted to turn

CHAPTER NINETEEN

things around and earn his salary, he needed to arrive much earlier and catch up on the rest.

As Frank pounded the little nails into the sole of the shoe he was working on, he thought about how much better things would be if he were the owner. There would never be a backlog. He'd see to that. No, he would stay up all night rather than allow things to get this bad. Keeping his customers happy, returning their shoes to them before they expected them, would be of paramount importance. And he'd make new shoes for customers, surpassing their expectations on quality and workmanship. That's where the real money could be made. Everyone always needed new shoes.

Smiling, he continued working until Jan stumbled through the front door in the late morning. As usual the man smelled of whiskey. His eyes were bloodshot as he took a sip from his pocket flask.

Jan came over to Frank, who was hunched over his worktable and reached out to rub his shoulders. Frank tensed and deftly slid away from the man's hands.

"Jan," he began, "today is payday."

"Yes, yes," Jan muttered, looking away. "At the end of day, I'll get you cash."

Frank let out a relieved sigh. He'd been worried when he realized how unproductive his employer had been. Did Jan actually have money? Customers wouldn't pay for work not done. The only comfort was that he always seemed to have a drink in his hand, so the man wasn't broke. Maybe all the work that Frank had been able to do was putting coins into Jan's pocket. Frank relaxed his shoulders. Yes, money must be coming in. Of course, he'd get paid.

Frank continued to work, avoiding Jan's wandering hands, which was a fulltime job in itself. Finally, when the bells of the church down the street chimed five o'clock, Frank turned the sign in the window to *Closed* and approached Jan.

He stood uncomfortably in front of his employer for a minute as the man just stared at him. Finally Frank cleared his throat and said, "Can I get my pay now? I have groceries I need to buy before I go home."

Jan glanced away and stood. He swayed slightly before he reached into his pocket and pulled out a small bit of lint. Laughing, he said, "Well, that's not it." Then he reached into the other pocket and pulled out a few crumpled bills. He flattened them out and counted them before handing them to Frank.

Frank took them, feeling a slight panic welling inside him. There was only ten dollars there. "Where's the rest?" he asked.

Jan shrugged and sat down. "It hasn't been a good week. Next week will be better. I can pay you more then."

"But you said you'd pay me one dollar thirty an hour. This isn't even one day! I need my pay."

Jan scowled at him. "This is all I have. What do you expect?"

Frank stared at him. "I expect you to pay me what I deserve."

"What's that?"

Frank looked at the scruffy man in front of him and wanted to kill him. Jan had lied to him. It was clear now. Jan had never intended to pay him anything. He was probably lucky that he got the ten dollars. What would Frank have done if there had been nothing but lint in his pockets?

He realized that there was no point in talking to the drunken man anymore. With a ragged sigh, Frank shook his head and left. The world spun slowly counter clockwise.

What would he say to Lanka? She was counting on him.

When he owned his own shop, he vowed to pay his staff generously. Only then would he find loyal, hardworking

CHAPTER NINETEEN

people. He had to figure out how to make his dreams a reality.

* * *

By the end of the following week, Frank found another cobbler looking for help—Alberto, of Alberto's Shoe Company. The wiry young man had taken over the business from his father, who had inherited it from his father. Alberto's had customers who had patronized this store for generations.

The position only paid ninety cents per hour, but it was clear that Alberto ran his shop with integrity. The shopfront was clean, and the owner was always hustling around the store, either helping a customer or working on a shoe in the backroom. No one ever waited long to be served.

Alberto's also had a large warehouse and more modern machines for making shoes than Frank had ever seen.

This was more like it. Frank was confident he'd be paid on time.

Lanka had been understanding about Frank's lack of money but was relieved when he got the new job. She would never complain, but Frank felt the pressure and didn't want to be a burden.

Now that he had a steady income, Frank could afford a new shirt, which he sorely needed, and could provide Lanka with good meat and fresh fruits. After a month, he felt he could finally relax and start to save.

He wrote to Ljubica, inviting her to come to Canada to be with him. He exaggerated his position a bit, but honestly said that he was earning enough money to support her now.

Frank told Ljubica how every day he worked eight hours in the shoe factory, making new shoes, and another three to four hours in the shoe repair department, keeping up with all the orders. Although there were a lot of cobblers in Toronto, no one had the level of experience, the number of machines, and the top-notch customer service as this shop. As a result, more people went to Alberto's for shoes.

Frank wrote about the production line; it had multiple stations manned by a host of interesting characters, some of whom had been in the business for years. He also wrote about how he'd learned to use the new machines. He felt lucky that they were willing to train him on these, as he would certainly need them in his shop when that time came.

He detailed one of the machines that was the most challenging for him, the toe lasting machine. There were three of these machines and one always seemed to need repair. This particular machine made him nervous. There were three adjustable pincers at the toe as the device pulled the leather up and over the toe. The difficult part came when he had to click a floor pedal as his fingers gripped either side of the shoe, angling it just so to clamp each pincer on the toe. The trick was knowing when to remove your hands, so your fingers didn't get caught. So far, so good, but he'd heard stories of people losing fingers, which made him very skittish about working with the machine.

Frank sent Ljubica a Polaroid photograph of himself, one that Lanka had kindly taken of him sitting on a boulder in a nearby park. She had borrowed the camera from the owner of the shop where she worked. He had been grateful for her help on a Sunday with the wedding party.

"Your girl should see what you look like," Lanka said with a smile as she smoothed a stray hair. "She won't be able to resist you."

Frank smiled. "She's not *my* girl yet."

"She will be," Lanka said confidently.

Two weeks later, Frank received a reply. Ljubica was still adamant that she couldn't leave Yugoslavia. Still, she did write back, and even across the distance he could feel that she was

CHAPTER NINETEEN

softening. He wondered if she somehow knew that he wasn't doing quite as well as he'd portrayed. However, that didn't stop him from continuing to write her at least once a month. And she always replied.

He'd find a way to convince her to come, one way or another.

Chapter Twenty

Spring 1958

The first thing Frank did when he was promoted to foreman at Alberto's Shoe Company was to write Ljubica. His hands trembled as he told her about his raise. He was now making two dollars and twenty-five cents an hour. It had been a little over a year and a half since he'd left Yugoslavia and he was finally making good money. And his competence in the shoe factory was unparalleled. He was no longer intimidated by the machines and could teach any newcomer how to safely operate them.

In each letter to his beloved, he shared his goals of owning his own business. It was clear that was the best way to make his fortune, but for now being a foreman was a good step toward that goal. Not only would he make more money, but he'd learn valuable management skills that would help him succeed later.

Surely his raise and continued dedication to his work would convince Ljubica to come to him. He didn't understand why she hung on to her life in Yugoslavia. He knew she had a few close friends, but her letters were always filled with stories about how difficult life was.

Ljubica kept telling him that she wasn't ready to leave. However, in her last letter, she also made it clear that she wasn't committed to any other gentleman. It was the first time she'd made such a declaration. Although she didn't say she wasn't

CHAPTER TWENTY

dating other men, it was clear that Ljubica was interested in Frank. For one thing, she always wrote him back.

Frank began to send her a few dollars with each letter, entreating her to buy flowers or chocolates or whatever she might like. If he couldn't be with her, he could at least shower her with the gifts that she deserved. She was his queen.

After a few months, Frank found a boarding house that offered him his own room with a bed. He broke the news to Lanka one evening.

"It's small," he said, "but it's a place I can call my own."

She stood mutely in front of him, just nodding. It was obvious to Frank that she was struggling to keep the tears from flowing.

"I'll be sharing a bathroom and a kitchen with two other families," he said, pointedly looking away, doing his best to ignore her sadness. He didn't want to see her cry.

He knew he'd miss Lanka, but he really liked the idea of having an actual door and privacy at night.

Finally Lanka found her voice. "It's a place that Ljubica might say yes to."

"Yeah, sharing a pallet on your floor wouldn't work. Not if we're going to start a family."

She beamed. "Invite me to your wedding?"

"Of course!" Frank said with a laugh. He was relieved that Lanka was no longer on the verge of crying. "But she never has given any indication that she'll come."

"Mark my words, boy. When you start your own company, she'll come."

He hoped she was right. Ljubica was probably waiting for him to make good on his promise to make a success of himself. After all, that's why he'd come all the way to Canada, risking everything that he had. He had no doubts that he could do it, but starting a new business from scratch was a challenge.

THE SOUL OF A SHOEMAKER

* * *

Frank thought about the best way to start his own business. He realized that he could perform every job at Alberto's shoe factory. The only problem was that he couldn't afford the expensive machines. Even second hand they were way out of his price range. So the solution was to open a small repair shop and build from there.

The next day, when Frank went to the factory, he looked around. He liked a lot of the men he worked with, but he needed to recruit one of them to be his partner. He knew enough to know it would be easier to start his own company if he didn't have to do it alone.

Frank had just a few candidates to consider. Rocco, a short Italian, who looked to be around forty years old, was never serious. Frank wondered if he even knew how to be serious—he was always joking around. It certainly lightened the day, but that wasn't what one was looking for in a partner. Plus, he didn't always get along with the others. Two stations down, Vuk, a beefy Russian, was an odd fellow. He seemed to have a cleaning fetish, as he was always sweeping and tidying. That would have been fine with Rocco, except that Vuk cleaned more than his own station. Rocco was territorial and would often wave his hammer at Vuk, voicing a lot of choice Italian phrases that no one in the room knew but all could guess. There were rumors of altercations after work, but Frank never witnessed them.

No, Rocco wouldn't work out.

Andrija was a tall and wiry Slovenian in his late forties. He drank a lot of coffee and always seemed to be moving in a blur around his station. The guy was a busy bee, working fast. Like Vuk, he always seemed to have a broom in his hand, sweeping up the staples that piled up. The problem with Andrija was that he loved to gamble. He spent a lot of

CHAPTER TWENTY

money on the lottery. One time he won a six-figure jackpot and promptly re-invested his winnings into more lottery tickets, which, of course, lost. Soon after, he'd approached Frank for a loan. No, Andrija wasn't a good choice. He was a nice guy, but he seemed destined to wind up murdered on the Toronto docks by a frustrated loan shark.

Again, not a great business partner.

Frank's eyes fell on Rikard. He was the only other Croat on the floor. The man was nearly one hundred and ninety centimeters tall and reminded Frank of a biker dude from the cinema. He rarely shaved and had thick, long black hair that he wore in a ponytail. To complete the look, he often had a cigarette hanging from his lips.

Despite his unruly appearance, Frank admired the man. For one thing, he had owned a restaurant in Croatia before he had defected. He knew what it took to keep the lights on and the customers happy. As it turned out, Rikard was a family man and not a rough-and-tumble biker. As Frank had gotten to know him, he discovered Rikard was nice and helpful; he was always willing to do what was needed to get the job done.

Frank nodded to himself. Rikard was a good choice.

After the workday, Frank cleaned up his station and wiped his hands on his pants. He walked by Rocco, who wore a deep scowl. He was glaring at Vuk, who was sweeping up Rocco's area with fervor. Vuk seemed to be blithely ignoring the death stares coming his way.

Frank shook his head and glanced at Rikard, who was still bent over his workbench. He nodded in appreciation of the workmanship on the shoe in front of the man. He waited until Rikard put the finishing touches on the brown loafer. It was only when he had finished that Rikard looked up into Frank's face and started slightly.

"Didn't see you there," he said.

Frank smiled. "Yeah, I noticed. Nice job."

Rikard raised an eyebrow. "How long have you been standing there?"

"Not long."

"You heading out?"

Frank nodded. "And you? I was hoping to talk to you."

Rikard blinked his eyes. "About what?"

Frank looked around and bent close to Rikard. "Let's go get a cup of coffee around the corner. I'll explain there."

Rikard stood up and grabbed his jacket. He looked around at the cluttered workstation and debris-filled floor and shrugged. "Vuk will handle it for me," he said with a grin.

Frank chuckled as he made his way to the door. Around the corner was a little diner where they still sold a cup of Joe for a dime, and it wasn't half bad. It was the perfect spot for a business meeting.

They sat in a booth and Rikard ordered a turkey sandwich and a Danish with his coffee. When the waitress left, Frank began.

"You and I, we know what it is to work hard," Frank began. "We didn't come all the way from Yugoslavia to work for a couple of bucks an hour."

Rikard nodded in agreement. "It's decent pay, but I agree. It's not what I had in mind. I'm making about the same as I was back home."

"Right. We're destined for more."

At least I am.

Again, Rikard nodded. "You have a plan?"

Frank smiled. "Not a plan exactly, but I want to start my own shop. Something small. Just repairs."

The waitress brought the coffees and left. Frank put a little cream in his while Rikard sipped it black.

"Do you have a store front in mind?" Rikard asked.

CHAPTER TWENTY

Frank shook his head. "Not yet, but I'm confident we'll find something. I've been able to save a bit."

"I saw a little shop for rent on Victoria Park and St. Claire. Maybe that would work?"

Frank felt his pulse quicken. His dream was quickly becoming an actuality. "That's great. Let's go take a look."

Rikard gave him a startled look. "But I just ordered."

"After."

"Sure. After."

Chapter Twenty-One

Alberto was sorry to see Frank and Rikard leave. Frank was relieved that his boss wasn't belligerent about it. Instead he said, "It's not easy starting up in this town. If it gets to be too much, you always have a spot here in my shop. You both are excellent workers. I'll be sad to see you go."

"Thank you," Frank said with a slight bow.

He had a momentary twinge of regret for leaving this place. He'd been there for over two years and enjoyed the work and people. Plus, he started having doubts, but quickly shook them off. No, this is why he'd risked everything to come to this land of opportunity. It wasn't to earn two-something an hour making shoes for someone else.

He and Rikard left quickly after saying goodbye to the rest of the crew. As they walked along the sidewalk, Frank realized that Rikard didn't have the same doubts that he did. He smiled. That was a good trait in a partner. He'd chosen well.

It didn't take them long to clean up the small shop and open the doors for customers. They couldn't afford a fancy sign, so they simply painted "Shoe Repair" in red block letters on a wooden board painted white. Together they hung it above the door.

After sitting in the empty shop for the better part of a day, Frank hopped off his stool so suddenly it startled Rikard.

"No one knows we're here!" Frank said in frustration.

Rikard remained seated. "So what do we do about it?"

CHAPTER TWENTY-ONE

"I don't know, but we need to do something." Frank began pacing back and forth in front of the counter.

"We can't afford advertisements."

"True. The question is, what can we afford?"

Frank looked out the door at the people passing by the store front. He walked to the door and started greeting people. Most were cordial and smiled back at him. Frank invited them to come in, but they all shook their heads. They had places to go, and no one needed their shoes repaired.

After an hour, Frank went back inside. "We need flyers."

Rikard snapped his fingers. "That's not a bad idea."

They bought sheets of paper and a couple of pens and began handmaking flyers. Frank wrote out ten before his hand started to cramp. He rotated his wrist in a few circles before he began again.

"Wouldn't it be nice if there was a way to make copies of these?" Frank said.

"There are machines that do that, you know."

Frank dropped his pen. "Oh, yeah?"

"I was reading about it last week. There's a new model coming out. It's called a Xerox."

"Where do we get a hold of one?"

Rikard laughed. "They're not available yet. Just a few prototypes. Besides, those things are huge, heavy, and expensive from what I understand. The magazine said that they might be available for purchase in a year or two, but only the big corporations will be able to afford them."

"Oh." Frank picked up his pen again and started writing out more flyers.

After a couple hours they had a few dozen. Some looked better than others, but in the end, if someone needed their shoes repaired, they probably wouldn't fault them for their penmanship.

Frank handed a few flyers out to passersby. Whenever someone dropped one on the ground, he'd pick it up, shake off the dirt, and reuse it. No sense in wasting the paper. They also went door to door within a radius of five blocks of the shop. A few people seemed interested, so Frank offered them a special deal if they came in that week.

Before long they had a few customers.

Word of mouth started to spread, and Frank made sure to take care of each customer as if they were a member of his family. As a result, more people came back to the little shop.

With excitement, Frank wrote to Ljubica. He sent her a Polaroid of him standing outside his new store wearing his best suit. He told her how he'd found a partner and the store had real potential for the future. He detailed to her various stories of his success, neglecting to mention the number of hours he and his partner were at the shop.

He also didn't share with Ljubica that he'd moved out of the new room in the boarding house to save a little money. He and Rikard decided to sleep on cots in the backroom of the shop. It felt like a step backwards, but he wanted to put everything into seeing this venture become a success.

Frank bit his lip as he penned the same request to his beloved. *Won't you come and move to Canada and be my wife?* He waited and waited for her to reply, waking up before dawn and closing the shop at night only after all the work was done. When he received the letter from Ljubica, he hesitated before opening it. As he touched the envelope, he thought about how her breath had caressed it as she licked it shut. It was as if she'd kissed it closed.

He smiled as he opened the missive and held his breath. She declined his offer once again.

Why? He'd done what he'd set out to do, hadn't he?

However, she left room for the possibility in the future. It kept Frank's hope up and drove him to work even harder.

CHAPTER TWENTY-ONE

He could picture Ljubica with a little baby in her arms and a toddler at her skirt. She'd make him delicious meals each night and talk with him about their day. He longed for her to change her mind and join him in Toronto.

As the year marched forward, Frank tried to hold on to his optimism, but all the money he plugged into the shop dwindled away. The fact was, there was only so much he could make repairing shoes. He always knew the real money would come when he could do what Alberto did and expand into manufacturing.

Sadly, it cost a lot of money to start a manufacturing company. They just didn't have the capital for the machines required, and making shoes by hand would be far too tedious and time-consuming.

Frank sat in the empty shop one swelteringly hot day, staring out onto the street, mesmerized by the passersby. The little fan in the corner barely moved the air around, and he could feel his shirt sticking to his back. He'd failed. No wonder Ljubica hadn't come. She'd known better than to risk everything to move to a new country and marry a man who'd just started his first business. Sure, he could talk a good game, but the reality was that he hadn't actually improved his condition. He was always struggling to make just enough money to keep up with all the expenses—there were many when you were the owner.

When Rikard came in toward the end of the day, he took one look at Frank and his shoulders slumped. They'd talked about shutting down the store a few times, but Frank could tell that somehow Rikard knew that this was it.

"Damn, but it's hot," Rikard said, looking away.

"Thirty-five at least."

"No customers today?"

Frank shook his head. "Nope, none. Only two yesterday."

"We could…" Rikard's voice trailed off as he watched Frank slowly shake his head.

"I'm sorry, my friend. It's just not going to work." He felt a heaviness in his heart that was hard to shake.

"What are you going to do?"

Frank shrugged. "Go back to Alberto's. What else?"

"Not me," Rikard said. "I decided that if you did quit, I'd move. I don't want to stay here forever working for someone else. I've got to try again."

Frank gave him a half-smile. He had to admire the man's energy and determination. Who knew, maybe Frank would get that feeling back again. "Where will you go?"

"Ottawa."

"Ottawa? What's there?"

If Frank were to be completely honest with himself, he had hoped that Rikard would stay in Toronto and go back to Alberto's with him. Frank liked the man and didn't want to see him go. There weren't many people that he'd become that close to in this city.

Rikard tilted his head. "I have a friend there. A Russian man who has been writing me almost every month. He started a little shoe repair store, kind of like ours; but it's doing better."

Frank felt the hairs on the back of his neck bristle, and he sat up straighter in his chair. "Oh yeah?" he said casually, hoping that Rikard didn't sense that he was just a little jealous. "So, your friend has been able to make it work?"

"Yeah," Rikard said, seemingly oblivious to his friend's irritation. "Boris said that he's been going strong for six months and that the money's rolling in. He wants to hire me starting at two dollars an hour."

"But that's less than Alberto's offering."

"I know," Rikard said with a sigh. "I just don't want to leave here and go back there, you know? It's too depressing. Besides, Boris said that if I do real well, I can earn more, maybe

CHAPTER TWENTY-ONE

even a percentage. Kind of like a partnership. He's also got an idea to expand the shop and maybe get a few machines."

"They're expensive."

"Boris says after two years in business, he thinks he can get a loan at the Royal Bank."

Frank scoffed. "Yeah, right."

Rikard crossed his arms across his chest and said, "I believe in Boris."

"But not me," Frank said, feeling unwanted emotions boiling up to the surface. He looked away to compose himself.

"*I'm* not the one wanting to quit!" Rikard said heatedly. "You're the one who's throwing in the towel."

"Yeah, well," Frank said, then stopped. He stood up and looked Rikard in the eye. Suddenly all his animosity left him, and he said, "Go. Do well. Keep in touch and let me know how it goes."

Rikard nodded his head. "Of course I will."

Chapter Twenty-Two

Frank easily found a room in a boarding house and applied for his old position. True to his word, Alberto took Frank back with open arms. Although Frank put a smile on his face every day and gave his boss everything he had, his heart just wasn't in it. He'd started his own business, he'd accomplished that goal and now he was back twenty steps, working for someone else, helping him make a profit and expand his business.

The year slogged by slowly. The workers in the factory performed their tasks just as they always did, day after day. He did the same. Nothing had changed.

Frank visited Lanka on the first Sunday of each month. She'd cook him traditional Croatian dishes, and they'd trade stories of their lives.

"When are you going to start another business?" she asked one day as she poured him a cup of coffee. "It's about time."

"I don't know," Frank replied, looking down at the last few bites of chicken on his plate. He moved them around with his fork. "What's the point?"

She frowned at him. "This is not the young man who knocked on my door three years ago! Who is this pitiful man who feels so sorry for himself?"

Frank looked into her eyes and sighed. "I grew up."

She scoffed. "Accepting failure isn't growing up."

Frank sat up straight. "I'm doing no such thing. I'm just not ready to start out on my own. I only have two thousand dollars saved."

CHAPTER TWENTY-TWO

Lanka whistled approvingly. "That's pretty good."

"Yeah, well I need very expensive machines. And starting money. And a larger facility so I can manufacture as well as repair shoes."

"So borrow the money."

"I need to figure out how much I need and who will lend it to me. I need to do some research."

"You can get what you need. Did you try the bank?"

Frank shook his head and pushed his plate toward the center of the table. "I doubt they'd loan money to me."

"You don't know until you try," Lanka said, her voice a little gentler. "You did so much to get here. I can't believe you're giving up."

"I am not giving up!"

"Good!" Lanka gave him a grin, and he realized she'd been goading him. She leaned back in her chair and gave him a knowing look. "Besides, Ljubica is pining away back in Yugoslavia, waiting for you to make something of yourself."

Frank's heart beat a little faster as he thought of her. How long would she stay single? It wasn't realistic for him to expect her to wait. With her beauty, she'd certainly have many suitors.

He nodded. "I'll go to the bank as soon as I can put some numbers together."

* * *

Frank threw himself into researching prices and looking at properties that might be suitable. Two weeks later, he left work a couple hours early. He walked straight to the bank and asked to speak with the manager. Frank had been a steady customer for the last two years, saving as much as he could.

After a twenty-minute wait, Mr. Clarke greeted him and invited Frank into his office. Frank looked around at the stately mahogany furnishings and the oil paintings on the wall. Mr. Clarke pulled out two Waterford crystal glasses and offered Frank cold water to drink.

After a few minutes of polite chitchat, Frank wiped his hands on his pants, looked Mr. Clarke in the eye, and gave the man his best pitch for loaning him the money to start his business.

To Mr. Clarke's credit, he heard Frank out and didn't interrupt him once. It was only when Frank was finished that Mr. Clarke said, "I'm sorry, Mr. Katana. It's just not possible."

Frank's shoulders slumped. "Why?"

"For one thing, you don't have any assets. Just the money you have in the bank, and that's not enough to borrow the funds you need."

"Experience is an asset."

Mr. Clarke gave him a sympathetic look. "Of course it is. But in order for us to loan you money, you need something a bit more tangible. You don't even own your own home."

"Do I need that?"

"No. But you need more than what you have."

"So what do I do?"

"Find a few partners. You don't need as much as some new businesses. I like your business plan. It's sound. Find likeminded men to help you get started."

Frank thanked him for his advice. He had to admit he felt a little better. Thanks to Mr. Clarke, he now had a plan of sorts. Upon consideration, he could think of three men he could approach to become partners. He didn't know them well because they tended to keep to themselves at Alberto's, but they came from the same province of Russia and shared the same Jewish faith.

After work the next day, Frank decided he had nothing to lose. He would talk to his prospects right then. As he walked over to their section in the rear corner of the shop, he slowed

CHAPTER TWENTY-TWO

his pace. What was he going to say to them? These three didn't know him and therefore probably wouldn't trust him. He turned to go back to his station and then chided himself for being silly. No, he needed to give this a chance.

He forced himself to turn back and when he was standing in front of the three, he asked if they'd meet him for drinks after work. To his surprise, they agreed. And they seemed happy that he'd asked them.

Smiling, he thanked them and returned to work, humming a little tune as he began to dream again about having his own company. Lanka was right. Now was a good time.

* * *

The small bar around the corner from Alberto's was packed with men and women blowing off steam after their workday. Frank waited for his eyes to adjust to the dim lighting. He then looked around, found a table in the corner, and signaled the three men to follow him. On the way, he ordered a pitcher of lager from the passing brunette waitress, who gave him a curt nod as she raced to clear off a table by the door.

As Frank waited for the beer, he sized up the three men. Yuri was a big bear of a guy. He always walked with a bit of a limp because his right leg was a little shorter than his left. To top it off, his shirt was usually stained and was rarely tucked in. Grigory, in contrast, was tall and slender and always wore a button-up shirt. Mikhail was the youngest and never quite looked you in the eye. He kept to himself.

Frank was pretty sure these men were all single. They appeared to prefer each other's company to those of a lady. He surmised that they likely had savings, since they didn't squander their money on lavish dates. He'd also heard that the three shared a flat and kept their costs down. They had a reputation for being frugal.

When the waitress brought four chilled mugs and the pitcher of lager, Yuri gave her a broad smile, then said in his baritone voice, "This is a good start, but you might as well bring a bottle of vodka. This beer is a good appetizer for the real stuff."

The other two laughed. Frank groaned inwardly. He hoped they didn't expect him to drink their vodka. If he started in on that, he knew he'd never make it into work on time the next morning. Besides, he much preferred Canadian Club Whiskey.

Frank took a swig of the beer, then wiped his mouth with the back of his hand. He put the mug down and said, "You probably wondered why I asked you here."

"Nah," Grigory said. "We don't need a reason to drink."

The three crashed their glasses together so hard in response that Frank half expected them to break. "Well, I did. Have a reason, that is." This wasn't going as smoothly as he'd hoped.

Just as Frank opened his mouth to discuss business, the waitress came back with four shot glasses and a bottle of Pearl Vodka, which sent up a cheer of approval from the three Russians.

The waitress began to pour, but Yuri swiped the bottle from her. "Don't worry, honey. I've got this. You run along and help your other customers."

The woman was off like a flash. Frank watched her go, thinking that she was pretty, but couldn't hold a candle to Ljubica.

Yuri sloshed vodka into the four glasses and onto the table. Knowing it was expected of him, Frank picked up a glass and downed it with them.

"Did I ever tell you about my time in the Russian ballet?" Yuri asked.

CHAPTER TWENTY-TWO

Frank suppressed a cough as the liquid burned the back of his throat. His face flushed and he set the glass down. "No, you never did."

Yuri went to refill it and Frank put a hand over the glass. "Hold on," he said. "I need to tell you something."

Yuri shrugged and filled the other three shot glasses. "Shoot. What you want to say?"

"Have you three considered starting up a business?" Frank asked.

Grigory slammed the vodka back, shook his head a few times, then said, "What kind?"

Yuri slapped him hard on the back with a loud laugh. "What kind of business do you think he means?"

"I don't know. Could be anything."

Yuri shook his head and let out a loud guffaw. "Maybe he wants to open a flower shop."

Grigory grabbed the bottle from Yuri and poured himself another glass, spilling an equal amount on the table. He chugged it and poured another.

Frank's eyes widened and he started to wonder if these three would make good business partners. Maybe for a bar, but not a shoe manufacturing plant.

Yuri put his glass down and turned to Frank. "You looking for partners?"

"Yeah," Frank said, taking a sip of his beer, "I am."

"Well now," Mikhail said, leaning in, "I think that's an interesting idea. Truth is, we have been talking about it."

Frank found that hard to believe. "You have?"

"Sure, why not?" Mikhail said. "We work hard, and we play hard. Isn't that right?" The last was aimed at his two comrades.

Grigory and Yuri nodded. "Yeah," they said in unison before they each chugged another shot.

Mikhail turned to Frank. "So you're looking to start a shop? Didn't you do that a year or so ago?"

"Yeah," Frank said. "It was just a little repair shop. I didn't have the capital to invest in the machines I need to make shoes, you know?"

Mikhail nodded. "We have some money saved. How much you figure you need?"

Frank looked around to make sure no one was listening. Talking about money in a public place like this might not be the best plan. However, their table was far enough away from everyone else that he figured it'd be all right. He lowered his voice and leaned in. "I've done some research. I figure we need twenty grand in startup capital. I have two, but think I can get three more, so I'm looking for fifteen on top of that. That would be five thousand from each of you."

Mikhail nodded, and without any hesitation and a wave of his hand he said, "We have that."

Frank stared at him. He hadn't expected the conversation to escalate so quickly and for it to travel in the direction he wanted it to go so effortlessly.

He leaned back in his chair and gave them a big smile. "Looks like I have some work ahead of me!"

Chapter Twenty-Three

January 1961

It took Frank six months to figure out how to start their new business and set it up. He approached the only person he knew who could help him to acquire the three thousand he needed to put up his stake in the business. Lanka. She had been saving her entire life and had a nice little nest egg. But would she be willing to invest in him?

"I'll pay you back within a year," he said.

"Of course, I'll invest in your business," she replied with a smile.

He grinned broadly and exhaled in relief. "Thank you. Thank you!"

Frank found a perfect little place. It was only twenty-five hundred square feet, but it was on Spadina Avenue in a very prominent area in the center of Toronto, just above Lake Ontario.

New machines were out of the question, but Frank managed to find a few old ones from a company going out of business.

The squat man with a long handlebar mustache frowned at Frank when he visited the shop to enquire about the three machines up for sale.

"Why would you start a new business now?" he barked. "It's a horrible time."

Frank held his tongue and managed to convince the man to give him a bargain. It wasn't as if there were many people knocking on his door ready to pay full price. In the end he spent a little less than what he had budgeted, and he knew his partners would be pleased.

Since this was such a big venture that included partners, he recognized that he needed help with the legal issues. A well-established lawyer, Mr. Martin, a man of medium build wearing a very nice suit, met with Frank and the partners on two occasions. In addition, Frank sat down with him a half dozen more times to settle the finer details. His partners didn't seem as interested in these elements, but Frank didn't want to take any chances.

There were times when Mr. Martin didn't charge him much for the visit. "I like to help new startups," he explained. "Besides, if you're successful, you'll be coming to me for all your needs."

Frank beamed. "Of course, I will."

"Have you considered a name?"

"No," Frank said with a sigh. "If I leave it up to my partners, they'll pick a Russian name."

"That might scare off customers," Mr. Martin said with a chuckle.

"Got any ideas?"

Mr. Martin scoured through a few books and said, "Looks like Celebrity Shoes hasn't been taken."

"Celebrity?" Frank liked the way the name rolled off his tongue. It conjured up images of beautiful women with diamonds and expensive clothes wearing his shoes. "I like it. Celebrity Shoes."

"You should run it by your partners quickly, and I'll double check to make sure that it's available. If all goes right, though, we have a name for your new venture."

CHAPTER TWENTY-THREE

That evening, Frank visited the partners at the local bar. They immediately agreed to the name.

"The ladies will think we're all celebrities!" exclaimed Yuri.

"Yeah, maybe they'll ask you to dance ballet," Mikhail said with a grin.

When Frank returned home, he took out a paper and pencil and began sketching ideas for a logo. He continued working at it until he found the right style. He drew a large "C" that curved under the rest of the word *Celebrity* written in cursive. Underneath, he wrote "shoes, ltd" in small letters.

"That's it!" he exclaimed to the empty room.

He was excited to show the sketch to the partners the next day. True to form, they glanced at it, shrugged, and said, "Sure. Why not."

* * *

Just after Frank signed the papers to start Celebrity Shoes, he wrote a letter to Ljubica, sharing with her the details of his plans. He included pictures of potential shoe designs and explained how Mikhail had experience designing women's shoes. They planned to have stylish pairs in the front window before long.

He sent the letter off and wondered if Ljubica would come to him. With this business, he knew he'd become a success. He had the capital to finally make his dreams a reality.

On the way back from the mailbox, Frank took a detour through the park. It was spring and a variety of flowers were in bloom. Their fragrance made him wax even more romantic. He imagined walking arm in arm with his wife here, maybe watching their young children play on the playground.

A cool breeze woke him out of his reverie, and he realized that he was making a lot of plans before getting a response from Ljubica. Up to now, she had never agreed to come. He continued to invite her, but she continued to reject him. What made him think that she would say yes this time?

As he continued to walk, he began to convince himself that she'd never arrive. She'd say no, just as she always had, and he'd have to face the fact that he'd need to find a wife here in Canada.

His shoulders slumped and he dropped himself onto a nearby bench just as the sun started to set. He didn't want a different wife. He wanted Ljubica.

The sun dipped below the horizon, and he realized that he'd put all his eggs in one basket and that basket might not be able to hold his life's dreams.

Wait for the letter, he chided himself. There was no need to expect the worst when the future was still unwritten. It was much better to spend his energies on becoming the sort of man that Ljubica would accept as her husband.

Think positively.

When Frank told Alberto that he would need to quit, his boss was happy to let Frank work until the last moment.

"Thank you for the forewarning," Alberto said. "Not everyone gives me notice. I hope that someday when you have dozens of workers, they will treat you with the same respect."

Frank nodded and realized there were a slew of new lessons he'd need to learn in the near future. He hoped life wouldn't throw them all at him at the same time.

* * *

When the letter from Ljubica arrived, Frank had a good feeling. He made himself a cup of coffee and sat at his little table. He could picture Ljubica sitting across from him, sharing breakfast.

He carefully opened the envelope and read the words that made his heart do cartwheels in his chest. She'd finally

CHAPTER TWENTY-THREE

accepted his proposal! She was coming to Canada as soon as she could. He couldn't continue reading, as the words were swimming before his eyes. He blinked back tears of joy.

When he had settled himself enough to continue to read, Frank learned that Ljubica was impressed with his new business. She made it clear that she felt he'd be a success. His heart swelled as he realized that she believed in him.

He quickly wrote her another letter and included five dollars for her to spend. He instructed Ljubica to start seeing what might be involved in getting a passport. The government probably wouldn't let her go without a fight.

Chapter Twenty-Four

Ljubica tried every channel she could to get a passport to leave Yugoslavia, but no one would approve one. Frank wrote her for months trying to come up with viable solutions. Then fortune smiled on them when one official whispered to Ljubica that the only way she could leave was if she were already *married* to a citizen of another country.

The solution became obvious: Marriage by proxy.

It wasn't an ideal situation, but it would work. Ljubica wrote how disappointed she was to get married that way. Frank's heart hurt when she confided her girlish dreams of a large wedding with bridesmaids. He smiled when he thought about the twenty-four-hour wedding celebration parties that he'd attended, where friends and family of the bride and groom would dance through the night celebrating the new couple with fervor.

Frank wrote her back and acknowledged that this was indeed a last resort. It wasn't as romantic as he would have liked, but it would accomplish the goal. They'd be married. And the government would not be able to stop her from flying to Canada.

He was glad he had the next day off so that he could visit Lanka and ask if she'd assist him in marrying Ljubica. He couldn't find a better woman to be her stand-in.

"I'd be honored," she immediately said with a sparkle in her eye.

CHAPTER TWENTY-FOUR

"Thank you."

"Come, have a seat. I'll make us some coffee."

When she brought out the tray, he noticed a plate of *kiflice*, little crescent cookies he hadn't seen in a long time. As he took a bite, powdered sugar fell on his pants leg, and he was instantly transported to his youth. Family picnics always featured these cookies, and his pants, shirt and face were often covered in a fine white powder.

Lanka took a sip of the strong brew, then asked, "How's Celebrity Shoes going?"

"Good," he said with an over-bright smile. The last thing he wanted to do was share all the trials and tribulations of the business.

Lanka rolled her eyes. "Franky, come on. It's Lanka. You don't need to pretend to me. I might be an investor in you, but I know what's it like starting up a new business. It's hard work. It's sweat and tears. It wouldn't be worth the effort otherwise."

Frank felt his shoulders relax. "My partners are only interested in making money. They don't seem to care about quality."

Lanka winced. "You mean they're cutting corners?"

"Yeah. They just want the cheapest materials."

"And you don't have a majority vote."

"No."

"Well," she began, as she took a bite out of a cookie, "It sounds like you need to buy them out as quickly as possible."

Frank nodded. "Agreed. But that will take some time."

She smiled at him. "I'm glad you have standards."

"That's the only way to really make it. Anyone can throw *sranje* at customers. But they won't come back if you do. People care about quality workmanship. They'll pay top dollar for shoes that don't fall apart on them."

THE SOUL OF A SHOEMAKER

* * *

Two weeks later, Lanka and Frank stood in front of a priest and exchanged vows. Frank looked into Lanka's eyes as he spoke his vows and he suddenly understood Ljubica's disappointment. How he wished it were Ljubica standing beside him. He longed to kiss her beautiful lips and embrace the love of his life.

He sent the marriage paperwork to Ljubica and asked her to find a proxy and get married. She wrote back that she did so at City Hall with a man who was the father of one of her kindergarten students. Frank grimaced as he thought about his Ljubica standing with another man. Did they kiss? He didn't like that she had looked into this man's eyes and had spoken the words she should have said to him.

He threw the letter down in frustration. He longed to feel Ljubica in his arms. Now. But still he had to wait. They were married, but he'd never even kissed his wife.

* * *

The next day when he woke up, he was not in a good mood. He called for a meeting with his partners, men he'd come to think of as The Three Stooges. They certainly didn't seem to care for much more than drinking and rarely came into the shop before ten.

Determined to make things work, he invited them to sit down around a small wooden table. They stumbled into their chairs, and he wondered if they were still drunk from the night before.

Frank looked each man in the eye, then turned to Mikhail. Out of the three, he was the most dedicated. "We need to make some changes."

Mikhail lowered his brows. "What kind of changes?"

CHAPTER TWENTY-FOUR

"I mean to make this business a success," Frank said. He took a deep breath and let it out. Then he forced a small smile on his face, one that he didn't feel. "Some of the shoes we're turning out aren't good. That's a sure way to fail."

Yuri waved a hand in front of himself. "Posh. You don't know what you're talking about. People buy our shoes. What does it matter?"

Frank stared at him. "It matters."

Grigori snorted. "What you're suggesting will cut into our profits. We're barely making anything as it is."

"It takes time," Frank said, trying to hold on to whatever patience he could. He felt his control slipping.

Again he took a deep breath, but before he could even let it out again, Yuri interrupted him. "You worry too much! Who cares if the shoes last the year. Better that they should break down. Then they'll come back to buy a second pair."

Yuri looked pleased with himself and the other two nodded and muttered their approval of his sentiments. Frank felt the last vestige of control slip away. He stood up suddenly and flipped the cheap table so that it pinned Yuri and Grigory to the floor. Mikhail had been on the end and jumped up, stuttering Russian words.

"What are you three blathering on about?" Frank shouted.

Yuri and Grigory stared at him wide-eyed from the floor, their mouths hanging open like fish that had been thrown out of the water onto land. Neither dared to speak. Frank glanced over at Mikhail, who stood with his arms crossed.

Pleased that none of them dared to speak, he continued in a soft, menacing voice, hoping it conveyed all the emotion that he felt. "Do you want me to get a gun?" he asked.

Yuri and Grigory looked at each other, then back at him. Neither said a word. They looked pale, and Frank could see Yuri's hand trembling.

Frank folded his arms across his chest. He gave them a severe look. "Because if you do," he continued, taking on a slightly crazed look, "I'd be *happy* to shoot all of you. And myself. That is, if we proceed *your* way. Might as well, because your way will bring us a slow, lingering death. And I'm not interested in that!"

He looked at them through slits. "Or we can do it *my* way!"

They all nodded so vigorously that he had to stifle the laugh that threatened to bubble up. He bit his lip and gave them a curt nod. "Fine."

The three partners still didn't say anything, so he left, not trusting himself to keep a straight face. He turned and closed the door behind himself, waiting a moment to see what they would do. All he heard was the furniture being set back up and a few muttered Russian phrases, which he was certain didn't paint him in a favorable light.

Chapter Twenty-Five

Frank stepped out of the shower and toweled himself off. His heart was racing. In two hours he'd see his beloved. He imagined that she'd be wearing a pretty, red dress with a matching ribbon in her beautiful brown hair. He had asked her not to bring anything with her. She was his responsibility now, and he wanted to fully care for her.

Ljubica had confided in him that all her clothes were old and well worn. She'd never miss them.

He arrived at the airport a full hour early. He'd purchased a bouquet of multi-colored flowers. It was Christmas Eve. He wished he could afford a decent present for her, but the flowers would certainly put a smile on her face.

As the minutes ticked by, his eyes remained glued to the gate entrance. Very soon she'd walk through the door into the airport and into his arms. His wife. He had a wife, and he was about to lay eyes on her for the first time in over six years. His heart began to beat out of control again.

Finally the plane landed, and it seemed like an eternity before the people started piling out. He watched as passenger after passenger walked through the door. A young brunette appeared, and his heart leapt into his throat before he realized it wasn't Ljubica. The woman quickly found and embraced an older man, who was probably her father. His eyes shifted back to the stream of people. Some were looking for their loved ones, while others walked directly to baggage claim.

When the flow of passengers trickled down to nothing, a few crew members exited the plane. He approached a blond stewardess. She was young and had a neat bob cut.

"Is everyone off the plane?" he asked.

"Yes, sir," she said. "Were you looking for someone?"

Frank felt as if the room was spinning around him. Why wasn't Ljubica on the flight? Maybe she'd changed her mind. No, that couldn't be. They were married. He looked at the kindly woman in front of him. "Yes, I am."

The woman gave him a sympathetic look. "She was coming from Frankfurt?"

"She started in Zagreb and should have changed planes in Germany."

"Ah," the woman said. "Let's see if something happened in Zagreb.

She took him over to an information desk and asked the man to see if Ljubica's flight from Yugoslavia took off on time. While the man picked up the phone to find out what happened, the blond stewardess said, "Perhaps she missed her connection and will be on the next flight."

Frank watched as the male attendant spoke in German to the person on the other end of the phone. After a few minutes, the man hung up the receiver. "I'm sorry, sir, but there's a very heavy fog in Zagreb. That plane couldn't take off."

"Oh," Frank said, feeling relieved. Ljubica hadn't changed her mind, after all. He felt lighter and his lips formed a wide smile. "That's great!"

The stewardess laughed. "It is?"

"Absolutely."

No need to explain. He thanked her and went home. Later that day he received a telegram from Ljubica explaining the situation. She'd waited in the airport for hours hoping the plane could take off, but the fog was so thick, she couldn't

CHAPTER TWENTY-FIVE

see anything in front of her. She said that the flight was postponed to New Year's Eve.

"A week away?" he muttered to himself.

The week passed by slowly. He tried to keep himself entertained and occasionally partook of a few shots of Canadian Club Whiskey and Coke to relax. He was so eager to welcome his new wife into his life.

What's one more week? he asked himself.

A long time.

Finally, when New Year's Eve arrived, he repeated the ritual and arrived early to the airport. However, when his beloved didn't walk through the gate door, he threw down the second bouquet of flowers and marched over to the same information desk. A different man was on duty, but he agreed to call to find out what happened.

"Sir, there is a fog in Zagreb. No flights could take off."

Frank practically growled at the man. "Another fog?"

He looked confused. "Sir?"

"I was here last week and was told the same thing."

"I don't know about that, but I do know that planes can't take off if the pilots can't see the runway."

Frank sighed and went home.

Alone.

Again.

He waited for the telegram to arrive. Ljubica let him know that she'd be there January 2nd. If there was no fog. He could hear the frustration in her words and somehow that gave him solace.

Well, January 2nd was two days away. He could make it until then.

* * *

As various families celebrated New Year's Day around him, Frank spent the day cleaning and recleaning the small room that was his home. Unfortunately, the tenants who shared the boarding house with him had spent the night drinking heavily. They had invited a few friends over to party with them, so the place was a mess. It took him the better part of the day to clean the shared kitchen and bathroom.

He was happy to have an activity to divert his attention from the next day; he felt as if his nerves were firecrackers ready to explode. With all this anticipation, he was ready to meet and truly make Ljubica his wife in every sense of the word. He had never dated anyone else. He'd always known she'd become his one day, even if she had been doubtful at times.

As the day came to a close, Frank was exhausted, partly from using muscles that he'd been unaccustomed to using while scrubbing and partly from his ragged nerves and unfulfilled dreams of what it might be like to hold Ljubica in his arms. He hardly slept a wink and, before he knew it, the sun was coming up.

Frank bounced out of bed and made himself a cup of coffee. He put two slices of bread in the toaster and waited. That was about all his stomach could handle. He glanced at his watch. She was due that midafternoon.

Not sure what to do with himself, he picked up a book, put it down, paced the small room, cleaned a little more, and then finally plopped down on a chair and stared at the ceiling for a while.

Later that morning, Frank looked out the window and saw it was sunny. He grabbed his warm coat and bolted out the door. He couldn't stand to be cooped up anymore. The cold wind made him pull his coat close, but he resolved to continue to walk. He headed to the park and saw only a few other people braving the cold. Finally, he walked back into the warmth of his room and waited.

CHAPTER TWENTY-FIVE

When the time came, he left for the airport with the flowers he'd purchased for Ljubica two days prior. He picked out two of the blooms that had begun to lose their freshness and nodded with satisfaction. She'd like them.

If she is actually coming.

Frank shook his head. No, she was coming. He wasn't going to allow for the chance that fate would intervene again. His nerves just couldn't take it.

He took his familiar station in front of the gate door and waited. As if willing the plane to land, he stared at the door and imagined what it would be like for her to walk through the doors and into his arms.

Finally, the plane landed, and Frank's heart began thumping so loudly that he was sure the man in the suit and tie next to him could hear it. His hand holding the flowers trembled as he continued to look at the closed door.

When it opened, and people started to come through, he carefully looked into each face. Not Ljubica. Not Ljubica. Not...

There she was. He'd have recognized her anywhere. As his beloved walked through the door, she scanned the crowd for him. Frank stood patiently waiting for her to spot him. Then she tucked a lock of hair behind her ear, and he realized she must be as nervous as he was. His hand stopped trembling.

Frank was happy to have the chance to feast his eyes on her for a moment before she saw him. She wore a rose-colored sweater that he was sure she'd knitted herself. It was perfection and showed off her tiny waist beautifully.

When her eyes lit upon his, the people around him seemed to move in slow motion. The only two people in the world that mattered at that moment were there. Frank finally was a few meters from the woman who was his life mate.

Ljubica gave him a little smile and walked toward him. He stood rooted to his spot, relishing the moment. When she came close enough, he enveloped her in his arms and kissed her with the passion he'd felt since the first moment he'd laid eyes on her in that park so long ago. She returned his kiss with a sweetness and openness that made him groan.

She was here.
She was his.
He was whole.

Chapter Twenty-Six

Frank took Ljubica home but could tell she was exhausted from her journey. With the patience of a saint, he didn't touch her that first night. He wanted their first time to be special.

The next night was. And the night after that. For the next two weeks, they didn't miss a night and Frank was in heaven.

Of course, there were a few changes he needed to make. For one, Ljubica insisted that he take a shower before he came to her each night. As a result, Frank was the cleanest he'd ever been in his life.

Three weeks later, Frank realized that she should probably be getting her monthly flow. At first when it didn't come, he felt fortunate. He didn't like the idea of being without her for three to five days. However, when another week passed and her period still didn't come, he asked her about it.

She shyly looked down. "It should have come by now."

He crinkled his brows. "So what does *that* mean?"

"I might be pregnant."

Frank pulled away from her abruptly. "Are you telling me that you came to me *pregnant*?" He felt a rage burning inside of him that started choking off his airways.

How could he have been so stupid? Of course she'd taken a lover, maybe two or more. She was so damn beautiful, it was naïve of him to think she had been truly chaste.

"No!" she cried. "Of course not. You were my first. You are the only man I have ever allowed to touch me."

"I don't believe you," he bit out. "It makes no sense."

"Don't you remember the first night?" she implored, reaching out to touch his arm.

He yanked his arm away from her so harshly she faltered backward a few steps to stop from falling over. "Of course I remember," he said through clenched teeth. "It was the happiest moment of my life. At least I *thought* it was."

She never looked away from him. "That night I bled. Remember?"

He couldn't remember much of anything at that moment. He was so mad. After all that, everything she'd put him through, Ljubica had betrayed him.

"Think!" she implored. "Think back. I bled because I was a virgin. I promise you."

He growled a guttural sound, then grabbed his coat and stomped out the door. He couldn't see straight. It was too much to bear. As he walked away, he could hear her plaintive cries following him down the stairs.

"Please, Frank, listen!"

He ignored her and walked to the door. Opening it, he grimaced as the cold air smacked him in the face. The wind chill was well below freezing. It wasn't a day to be outside, but he didn't care.

As he walked briskly around the block, he thought about his friend, Roko. He'd married a girl only to find out she was pregnant with someone else's child. To his credit, he didn't kick her out, but he'd complained bitterly to Frank whenever they got together. Frank had been horrified that anyone could be that deceptive to someone she claimed to love.

He stopped in the middle of the sidewalk and looked back toward his boarding house. Could his sweet Ljubica be that deceitful?

No. With a blinding insight he realized that she wasn't that other girl.

CHAPTER TWENTY-SIX

Suddenly, he remembered the blood that had stained his sheets that first night. He stopped moving for a moment as the world tilted crazily around him.

What had he done?

He raced back up the stairs two at a time and burst through the front door. Ljubica was sitting in a chair, quietly sobbing. He grabbed her. "Are you telling me the truth?" he demanded, pulling her chin up to make her look at him. Her beautiful, brown eyes gave him his answer. Frank instantly knew she was being honest.

He pulled her into a strong embrace before she could answer. "I'm sorry," he whispered into her ear. "I'm sorry I doubted you, my love."

"It's fine," her muffled voice replied. She sounded relieved. She pulled away and looked up at him. "When I came to you, I was most fertile."

He nodded but didn't completely understand. "All right."

She laughed and said, "A woman is most fertile in the time between her periods. We were very fortunate, my husband. Most couples have to wait much longer to have children. We are blessed."

He smiled at her. "We are, indeed. Very."

* * *

The next six months flew by quickly. Ljubica's pregnancy went well despite the intense morning sickness she experienced in her first trimester. The doctors had offered her a prescription of Thalidomide, but she didn't trust it, and Frank agreed. Why mess with nature?

Frank was determined to catapult his business to a new level. He had a family to support and planned to have another child as soon as they could manage it. If he was going to make Celebrity Shoes a booming enterprise, he had to get rid of

The Three Stooges. They'd never see eye to eye about how to run the shop. He needed fifteen thousand to buy them out. Fortunately, they didn't seem eager to stay, as they were tired of Frank's insistence on quality over cost.

Every penny Frank made he plugged back into the business, but he also started putting some aside to pay off the partners. He had five thousand saved. He needed another ten.

"Why don't you go to the bank?" Ljubica said one evening as she ladled some venison stew into a bowl.

He tore off a piece of dark pumpernickel bread that she'd just baked and dipped it into the bowl. He closed his eyes with pleasure at the taste. Boy, could she cook tasty meals, and on only five dollars a week. "I tried that once."

"But not recently. Celebrity Shoes has been going strong for nearly a year. You should reapply, my husband."

"I could," he said, mulling over the idea. She was right, they had some assets now and a bit of a track record. He smiled at her. "All right, first thing Monday morning."

When Frank sat down with the bank manager, he was surprised that the man didn't immediately say no. In fact, he gave Frank all the paperwork and asked what he wanted to borrow.

"Ten thousand," Frank said.

"I can get you twenty-five."

"Are you serious?"

"Celebrity Shoes has a good location. You have a good reputation and three full-time employees. You've done well in a short period of time."

That night Frank celebrated with his wife, whose belly was bulging. He still had niggling doubts that the child was his, but he pushed those thoughts away. Either way, he'd raise the son or daughter as if it were his. That was a certainty.

"I bet it was your confidence that won him over," Ljubica said proudly.

CHAPTER TWENTY-SIX

He grinned at her. "I bet it was."

* * *

It was a cool October afternoon when Ljubica went into labor. Frank raced around their new two-bedroom apartment like a wild man, throwing things into a small suitcase.

"Why didn't we pack beforehand?" he muttered.

Ljubica smiled through the pain as she sat in a chair waiting for him to take her to Toronto General Hospital.

When they arrived, the staff shoved paperwork at them. Ljubica couldn't speak a word of English and Frank didn't understand the language well enough to decipher what the forms said. He could speak English, but reading these documents was another matter.

When a loud, anguished cry ripped from Ljubica, Frank told her, "Just sign them. We can't delay anymore."

She did so, and they were whisked into a room. She winced as she was put on a cold table. Various doctors and students came by to poke and prod at her.

"What's going on?" she whispered.

"I don't know. Maybe it was those forms you signed."

"You mean I gave permission to allow all these people to come and go?"

Frank shrugged. Honestly, he didn't care as long as they made sure his child was born healthy, with ten fingers and ten toes. Even nine would be acceptable.

After a few hours, the doctor nodded to Frank and moved into position in front of his wife, encouraging her to push. Within minutes his little daughter was looking up at Frank with eyes that matched his perfectly—crystal blue. He ran a gentle finger through her beautiful black hair. He laughed.

"You're mine, little angel," he whispered as he leaned down to kiss her brow, taking in her wonderful scent. "You're truly mine."

Over the next week, he visited his wife and newborn in the hospital every day. It was a crowded room, filled with other families. One woman had just delivered her seventh child. He waved at the woman, who smiled in return.

Ljubica pulled Frank close. "That lady over there," she whispered, indicating the woman he'd just greeted, "asked me if I'd trade children with her! Can you believe that? Apparently, she's been hoping for a girl."

"She couldn't have been serious," Frank said, looking back in her direction. She looked tired. He looked back at his wife. "She couldn't have meant it. Could she?"

"She did. Seven boys. She delivered seven boys and sorely wants a girl."

Frank shook his head. "What did you tell her?"

"I told her that would never happen. What nerve!"

Frank glanced back at the woman and saw that she was fast asleep. He imagined that the woman was probably grateful for the bit of rest the hospital visit offered. He smiled down at his wife, whose eyelids were starting to droop.

"Go to sleep, my beloved. You deserve it."

Chapter Twenty-Seven

September 1967

"Susan!" Ljubica called down the stairs. "Come help me decide which dresses to bring."

"Can we go to the park?" Susan asked.

"Maybe later. We have a lot to do before we leave tomorrow."

"OK, *Majka*."

Frank's heart stirred as he watched his four-year-old daughter bound up the stairs. So much energy in that one. After they packed, he'd take her to the park to run around a bit.

"*Majka!*" little Frank junior called from the bottom of the stairs.

Frank scooped up his son in his arms. "You want to go see your *Majka*?"

The little boy nodded happily, so Frank climbed the stairs to the upper landing. He paused there for a moment and looked around. Two years prior Celebrity Shoes had taken off, and just after his baby son came into the world, he was able to put a down payment on their three-bedroom home in the lovely community of Scarborough.

It felt good to be able to provide a little luxury for his bride and children. When he'd purchased it, Ljubica had planted a kiss on his lips, looked him in the eye, and said, "I always believed in you."

He grinned. "You certainly motivated me to reach new heights."

"That's my job, isn't it?"

"Absolutely."

As he continued to reminisce, Frank junior became impatient at being held so long and squirmed to be let down. Frank complied, and the boy immediately scampered off to his sister's room to help them pack.

Watching his son run off, he sighed. It would take at least a half a day to get to Zagreb, where he'd meet his sister, Mila, for the first time since that day he left Mali Bukovec. With the change of planes and a layover in Bern, Switzerland, he wondered how they'd keep the two little ones entertained. They'd manage one way or another. After all, other families did.

Frank peered into Susan's room, which was in a state of upheaval. All her clothes were strewn across her little bed and Susan was kneeling in the center, as if directing traffic.

"That one," she said, pointing to a pretty white dress with buttons down the front. "And that one. And that one."

"Yes," Ljubica said. "These will be good. The white one will be good for the event."

"What event?" Susan asked.

Ljubica looked up at Frank with pride. "Well, your father is donating a brand new fire truck to the brave men of the Mali Bukovec fire department. They want to celebrate."

"Mali Bukovec!" Frank junior repeated with an enthusiastic chirp, having recognized the name. He was proud that he could pronounce the name of the village so clearly.

"That's right," Ljubica said as she clapped her hands. "Such a good boy."

Frank smiled. Together, they made sure to teach their children English but kept the Croatian language alive in their household. Frank wanted to make sure his children knew their roots. This trip would certainly help with that

CHAPTER TWENTY-SEVEN

goal. Then when they grew older, he'd make sure they spent more time there.

"What kind of truck?" Susan asked. "Is it big?"

"Yes," Frank said, feeling a surge of pride. "It's brand new and bright red."

It seemed like yesterday that he'd been back in Croatia helping the other volunteers use the antiquated hand pump to put out fires. Since that time, the brigade had been able to scrape together the money needed to get a real fire engine. However, that one was second hand and in sore need of repairs. Those men worked so hard to keep the countryside safe from fires; it was the least he could do to send them money and purchase decent equipment.

"Will I see it?" Susan asked, excitement flooding her little face.

"Of course!" Frank said. "And maybe you can get a ride in it!"

Susan cheered loudly, jumping up and down on her bed. Frank junior climbed onto the bed, whooping, hollering, and jumping with her. He always tried his best to outdo his sister. Ljubica and Frank looked at each other and broke into laughter. These two children truly made their lives complete.

* * *

Frank and his family walked down the center of the main street of Mali Bukovec at the head of the volunteer fire department. The two dozen men were decked out in freshly pressed uniforms and obviously proud to walk alongside their main benefactor. Every few minutes an enthusiastic member of the brigade broke ranks to run up to Frank and thank him for his ongoing support and donations.

People streamed from their homes and shops to cheer him and his family. Frank, wearing a tuxedo, held the small hand of his daughter. She, in turn, held his gorgeous wife's hand. Frank junior scampered beside Ljubica. Both children wore the official hats given to them by the chief. They seemed a little overwhelmed by all of the attention, but took it in stride, waving at the enthusiastic crowds lining the streets.

Frank felt tears well up and did his best to master his emotions. He didn't want to break down in front of all these people. He'd expected that the fire department would present him with a plaque, but he never thought they'd throw a full parade in his honor. He felt as if he was a royal dignitary, visiting from a far-off land.

Frank took it all in and smiled at Ljubica. This was his group, his family. He couldn't be prouder.

After all these years, it was good to be home.

Acknowledgements

The world is a better place thanks to immigrants like my father, Frank Katana, who came to a new country to work hard and help others along the way by sharing their wealth through the kindness and goodness of their hearts with no expectations in return.

Writing a book about the story of my father's life was a surreal process. When I started this project, my dad was diagnosed with Alzheimer's/Dementia. I am forever indebted to my family and friends for their ongoing support in bringing my dad's stories to life. Because of their encouragement, I have a legacy to pass on where one didn't exist before. I am eternally grateful for my family and friends who supported me and encouraged me to publish my dad's story.

This book was researched over the years, extrapolating from family stories told over dinner parties, trips to my parent's home, and summer vacations to Croatia during my childhood.

I want to acknowledge the outstanding debt I owe my parents, Frank and Ljubica. If it were not for them, I would not be here. You have taught me discipline, tough love, respect, and so much more that have helped me succeed in life and made me the remarkable entrepreneur, wife, and mother I am today.

To my mother, Ljubica, I love you. I cherish the many times you told me your life stories from your time at the orphanage, all the adventures you experienced, especially how you and dad met, and dad's determination to not give up on you.

To my father, Frank, thank you for your love and support. I will never forget the first time you told me you were proud of my accomplishments after I had graduated from high school with honors and scholarships while we were sitting in a bar in Pompano Beach, Florida. You were drinking your favorite CC and coke, and I was so stunned by your revelation that you left me speechless. You are a visionary and a brilliant entrepreneur. Your hard work, perseverance, and generosity have touched so many people over the years. We appreciate everything you have done for us, and we love you. That's all that matters.

And to my brother, Frank Jr., I am forever grateful for the hours you spent gathering family records and photos, writing and telling me some of dad's exciting stories. Those efforts helped bring this memoir to life. I am thrilled your lovely wife Annalie and your most adorable son Cristoff are part of our small, but a force to be reckoned with, family.

To Frank's sister, my aunt Mila Gruden, who painstakingly took the time to email me many fascinating stories about my dad and their family life on the farm. The emails were written in Croatian, but that was ok as it made me think twice as hard after I translated them, even if it may or may not have made any sense to me. And to all my cousins, aunts, and uncles in Croatia, I miss you all, as we have not traveled back home in many years.

The assistance provided by my awesome friends, Christina and Lisa, is greatly appreciated. From reading my final draft, giving advice, and being there for me. Thank you to all my Facebook family and friends. Your comments were on the mark, and I appreciate you. Special thanks to Laura, who made this book eminently more readable than it otherwise might have been. And a significantly extra special thanks to

ACKNOWLEDGEMENTS

Amy, Alexandra, and Connor, and of course, Captain, because I love you all so much!

And to my dear mother-in-law Genia. I miss you. You were my critiquing English professor when I registered for a few online creative writing classes. Sitting across the kitchen table, I would read to you my assignments, but then you would tell me about your stories, which were just way more interesting. You inspired me, and I will never forget you.

I'm immensely grateful to my neighborhood tribe. Marina, thanks so much for always being around. Ioana, thank you for suggesting I join your book club. You are all awesome, bringing me happiness and joy when we get together. I am lucky to have such wonderful friends and workout groups just around the corner, and thankful to have you all in my life!

A special thanks to my ever-patient husband, Stuart, and our two extraordinary sons, Andrew and Bradley. You inspire me to be my best, and I will forever be grateful. You kept me busy during the lockdowns and from going bonkers with all the drama. Without you, this book would not have been possible. I am thankful to you.

To all the individuals, friends, acquaintances, and random strangers I had the opportunity to discuss, comment on, or commiserate with about my book's progress, I want to thank you for your patience and understanding. I finally did it!

About the Author

Susan Cork worked as a freelance graphic and WordPress designer. Over the past 20 years, she has developed and managed websites for small businesses and large corporations. In 1998, she became a member of the accredited Association of Registered Graphic Designers of Ontario.

Susan designs and sells digital products on Amazon and POD Print on Demand sites. Susan has also published planners, journals, and storybooks with KDP under her trade-marked brand, Adam and Marky®, and Ginzburg Press. She lives in Markham, Ontario, with her husband Stuart and two sons: Andrew and Bradley.

Connect at SusanCork.com

www.ingramcontent.com/pod-product-compliance
Lightning Source LLC
LaVergne TN
LVHW021819060526
838201LV00058B/3441